Straddling Economics and Politics

Cross-Cutting Issues in Asia, the United States, and the Global Economy

Charles Wolf, Jr.

RAND

This publication was supported by RAND using its own funds.

Library of Congress Cataloging-in-Publication Data

Wolf, Charles, 1924–
    Straddling economics and politics : cross-cutting issues in Asia, the United
States, and the global economy / Charles Wolf, Jr.
        p. cm.
    "The 38 essays in this book were written between the end of 1996 and the
middle of 2001, and published in the Wall Street journal, [et al.]"—Forward.
    "MR-1571."
    ISBN 0-8330-3181-3
    1. Globalization—Economic aspects. 2. Globalization—Political aspects. 3. Free
enterprise. 4. International economic relations. 5. United States—Economic
policy—1993–2001. 6. United States—Economic conditions—20th century. 7.
United States—Politics and government—20th century. 8. Financial crises—Asia.
9. Asia—Economic policy—20th century. 10. Asia—Economic conditions—20th
century. 11. Asia—Politics and government—20th century I. Title.

HF1359 .W653 2002
330.9—dc21

                                                                        2002069746

RAND is a nonprofit institution that helps improve policy and
decisionmaking through research and analysis. RAND® is a
registered trademark. RAND's publications do not necessarily reflect
the opinions or policies of its research sponsors.

Cover design by Maritta Tapanainen

Published 2002 by RAND
1700 Main Street, P.O. Box 2138, Santa Monica, CA 90407-2138
1200 South Hayes Street, Arlington, VA 22202-5050
201 North Craig Street, Suite 202, Pittsburgh, PA 15213-1516
RAND URL: http://www.rand.org/
To order RAND documents or to obtain additional information,
contact Distribution Services: Telephone: (310) 451-7002;
Fax: (310) 451-6915; Email: order@rand.org

The 38 essays in this book were written between the end of 1996 and the middle of 2001, and published in *The Wall Street Journal, The Asian Wall Street Journal, The Wall Street Journal Europe, The Los Angeles Times, The New York Times, The International Herald Tribune, The Weekly Standard, Critical Review, Society, The Milken Review,* and *International Economy.* All the essays appear in their original, unedited form, and none has been altered in light of the world-shaking and world-shaping terrorist attacks of September 11, 2001 on the World Trade Center in New York and the Pentagon in Washington, D.C. Two of the essays (Chapter 29 and Chapter 35), although written in 2001, weren't published until early in 2002.

Most of the cross-cutting issues dealt with in these essays are as pertinent in the post– as in the pre–9/11 environment. Whether globalization is good or bad and for whom, how to measure it or how to influence it, remain timely questions now as they were then. The admission of China and Taiwan to the World Trade Organization (WTO), and the economic and other consequences of this change in status, will continue to be of regional as well as global significance. So, too, are issues addressed in other chapters, including the case for and against a "new international economic architecture," the outlook for a strong or a weak euro, the ramifications of China's continued if fitful progress toward capitalism, and the "fairness" and other effects of changes in U.S. marginal tax rates or in government spending as central elements in U.S. fiscal policy.

As indicated by this snapshot of the book's contents, the subject matter covers a wide range of disparate issues, reflecting matters I have been interested in during this period. I have organized the chapters into three parts to provide a semblance of cohesion:

I. *The Global Economy,* which includes chapters dealing with globalization, financial crises, WTO, and the euro;

II. *The U.S. Economy and Foreign Policy,* which includes essays on U.S. tax cuts, the trade and budget deficits, and whether and when it makes sense for the U.S. military to intervene abroad; and

III. *Asian Economics and Politics,* which comprises most of the book's chapters, spanning a wide range of topics from "Asian values" and whether they differ from "western" ones, to economic forecasts for the Asian region, to Asia's recovery from the 1997–1998 financial crisis, and to numerous country-specific issues involving China's economic growth, cross-Strait relations between the mainland and Taiwan, Japan's economic stagnation, and the eventual costs of Korean reunification.

Bridging this assortment of subjects and partly connecting them are several prominent, cross-cutting themes.

First, the author is a strong, but not uncritical, adherent of free and competitive markets, and of market mechanisms rather than government intervention to address economic problems. This theme occurs and recurs in the three parts of the book in describing various issues and in evaluating policy measures to deal with them. However, this stance does not proceed from a belief that markets, when left to their own devices (e.g., "laissez-faire"), always manifest the full range of attributes associated with perfect markets, to wit: full and free competition; symmetric information available to buyers, sellers, and potential competitors as well as current producers; generally rising cost curves notwithstanding economies of scale and scope; and so on. Indeed, it is typically the case that some of these attributes are missing from real-world markets. Instead, my support for market mechanisms derives from an empirically based belief that the evident shortcomings of markets are frequently overbalanced by the often neglected, overlooked, and unacknowledged drawbacks of government efforts to redress the market's shortcomings.[1]

This theme recurs in Chapters 3, 4, 5, and 6 dealing with financial crises, the International Monetary Fund, the problem of "moral hazard," and the continuing clash between reliance on markets or on government intervention. The theme also appears in Chapters 24, 25, 27, 28, and 29. dealing with the Chinese economy, its prospects, and its fitful march away from central planning and toward capitalism; in Chapter 10 where a rebuttal is presented to George Soros's alarmism about "market fundamentalists" and his predicted collapse of the global capitalist system; and in Chapters 32, 33, 34, and 35 dealing with Japan's economic malaise and possible remedies for it.

A second theme evident in several parts of the book is a pervasive skepticism and criticism of U.S. efforts, however well intentioned, to intervene in politically-charged, ethnically-complex, and murky conflict environments, (such as Bosnia and Kosovo), along with pessimism about whether the expected good resulting from such efforts exceeds a reasonable prognosis of the harm inflicted by them. (As suggested earlier, this view would warrant reappraisal in the post–September 11, 2001 environment—a reappraisal not attempted in this book.) The theme is also manifested in Chapter 37 dealing with the costs of Korean reunification if and when it occurs, and how to effectuate it without such large foreign subventions to North Korea as have been urged by others. Instead, I suggest that emphasis should be placed on a more austere, closely monitored, *quid pro quo* negotiatory and enforcement stance.

Third, and seemingly inconsistent with the preceding theme, is a more activist inclination toward restarting cross-Strait discussions between Mainland China and Taiwan. This theme appears, for example, in Chapter 30, dealing with "One China and *Three* Systems," and Chapter 31 on restarting discussions between the two WTO parties. The reason I characterize this as only "seemingly" inconsistent, rather than blatantly inconsistent with the anti-activist position referred to earlier, is that the concrete policy suggestions offered in

---

[1]For an exposition and elaboration of the theory and evidence underlying this position, see Charles Wolf, Jr., *Markets or Governments: Choosing Between Imperfect Alternatives*, MIT Press, 1993.

these chapters do not specify how much of a role the United States should play in this process. To be sure, this is a bit disingenuous since the likelihood that the parties would actually do something along the lines I suggest without an explicit and committed U.S. initiative may be small. Attempting to reconcile my general aversion to interventionism with this inclination to exert influence in tension-easing directions in the case of China and Taiwan would at best be labored. Suffice it to say that, at least in this instance, I agree with Emerson's dictum that "foolish consistency is the hobgoblin of little minds"!

Fourth, several of the chapters try to envisage the economic and military directions in which particular countries or regions are moving, and what the movements portend for the future. Sometimes this takes the form of formal economic forecasts, as in Chapters 17, 18, and 19, in which forecasts are made for the principal Asian countries of four key variables: gross domestic product (GDP), per capita GDP, military spending, and the accumulation of military capital. Based on these forecasts, comments are made about the Asian political and security environment that may result from these trends. Underlying the formal forecasts is a premise that two of the critical ingredients of national power, and the relative stature and influence of countries, are their economic size and growth, on the one hand, and their military capabilities, on the other. While these are certainly not the only ingredients of national power, they are among the most salient as well as the most calculable ones. Elsewhere in the book, the forecasts that appear are of a more qualitative and at least equally conjectural sort, as in Chapter 33's and 35's assessment of Japan's long term prospects, and Chapter 26's speculation about whether a freely and fully convertible Chinese yuan would be more likely to trade at a depreciated or appreciated rate against the dollar.

Finally, I should acknowledge that some of my views that seemed on track at the time they were expressed have turned out to be wide of the mark when the future they were envisaging actually arrived. One example: Chapter 13 expressed doubts that the consensus estimates of a prospective ballooning of the U.S. trade and current account deficits would materialize. Well, the consensus was correct; my doubts proved to be wrong. Another example, Chapter 15, dealing with taxes, trade, and growth in 1996, analyzed the savings-investment imbalance in the United States by principally emphasizing the insufficiency of domestic savings, rather than the excess of investment. In hindsight, the investment boom and its excesses in the late 1990s in fact led to domestic excess capacity and the recession of 2001. So, while my crystal ball helped in some cases (many relating to Asia), it obscured in others (several relating to the United States!).

I have always believed that commentators—whether of a scholarly or more journalistic bent—should be held to account for their pronouncements. Whether such accountability through some type of scoring system is provided by others or even by themselves, it has seemed to me that it would serve a useful purpose by discouraging hype and encouraging responsibility. With this aim in mind, I have added a brief "Postaudit" at the end of each essay, indicating whether, in my judgment, the essay seems currently to be valid and relevant compared to when it was written. In my scoring system, 23 of the essays stand up to this test quite well (each receiving an "A" or "A–"), ten warrant B's (meaning they do passably well), and five receive C's, which means they fail to make the cut! For those readers who might be interested in the finer-grained evaluation, I did best on Parts I and III—on the global economy and Asia, respectively—and least well on Part II, dealing with the U.S. economy. The record is not as good as I would have liked, yet better than that of such soothsayers as George Soros, Robert Mundell, Paul Krugman, Fred Bergsten, Jean-Claude Trichet, and several others mentioned in these essays.

Charles Wolf, Jr.
Santa Monica, CA

CONTENTS

FIGURES

TABLES

Part I

The Global Economy

Chapter 1

GLOBALIZATION: MEANING AND MEASUREMENT[1]

1. Rhetoric and Spin

Millions of words have been written, hundreds of conferences convened, and dozens of books published about globalization. Yet the subject remains clouded, if not obscured, by the rhetoric surrounding it.

The situation recalls a comment by an 18th century philosopher, sometimes referred to as the "first American." Said Benjamin Franklin (I paraphrase slightly): Where there is "a flood of words," there is usually only "a drop of reason."

Or, to cite an anonymous 17th century poet: "Where words most abound, much sense beneath is rarely found."

As a result of the rhetoric, media hype, and spin associated with globalization, as well as the occasionally violent demonstrations against it, globalization has become a convenient scapegoat for many things—indeed, for almost anything, and sometimes seemingly for everything. Globalization has been blamed for the Asian financial crisis of 1997–1998, the Russian economic plunge in 1999, global warming, hormone-treated beef, the spread of foot-and-mouth disease in Europe, and even piracy in the South China Sea!

A slightly edited version was published in **Critical Review** *on April 30, 2001 under the same title.*

[1]Based on a presentation originally made at the 3rd annual conference between RAND and the China Reform Forum, held in Beijing in November 2000, on *The Challenges of Globalization.*

The phenomenon recalls the role of the Vietnam war as an all-purpose scapegoat for anything that went wrong in the 1960s and 1970s: stagflation in the United States, the drug culture in the United States and Europe, even the sharp increase in teenage pregnancy in the United States.

Use of the term "scapegoat" doesn't mean that globalization has had no contributory responsibility for any of the untoward developments mentioned above. But in each case the predominant causes and responsibilities lie elsewhere. For example, the Asian financial crisis was mainly caused by misguided policies, especially by maturity mismatches between the terms on which funds were borrowed and those on which they were invested, rather than by anything properly attributable to globalization.

2. What Does It Mean?

The word has been used in so many different contexts, and with so many different connotations, that it recalls Humpty Dumpty's pronouncement: "When I use a word it means just what I choose it to mean—neither more nor less." Still, it would seem desirable to arrive at a reasonably clear definition of globalization before considering how to measure it.

At a simple, dictionary level, globalization is defined as "The act, process, or policy of making something worldwide in scope or application." Before dismissing this definition as too simplistic, it is worth recalling an observation by Ernest Rutherford that unless you can state a technical point in simple, non-technical language, you probably don't really understand it!

Other definitions include the following, more or less in order of increasing complexity:

> "[Globalization is] the intensification of worldwide social relations...in such a way that local happenings are shaped by events occurring many miles away." (Anthony Giddens, 1990)

> "Globalization reflects a more comprehensive level of interaction than in the past, something different from the word 'international.' It implies a diminishing importance of national borders and the

strengthening of identities...beyond those rooted in a particular region or country." (Ford Foundation Report, 1997)

"Globalization is the growing economic interdependence of countries worldwide through the increasing volume of cross-border transactions in goods and services and of international capital flows, and also through the more rapid and widespread diffusion of technology." (International Monetary Fund, 2000)

"Globalization is not a policy option, but a fact...The emerging reality is that all nations' militaries are sharing essentially the same global commercial-defense industrial base." (Donald Hicks, Defense Science Board, 2000)

The first three of these quotations are representative of many generic definitions, while the fourth has a more distinctive, and perhaps slightly paradoxical, quality. The paradox is that, while proclaiming globalization as a "fact" and not a "policy option," its focus on the "emerging reality" of a "shared global commercial-defense industrial base," actually opens up a wide range of differing policy options: for example, easing or restricting controls on the export of military or dual-use technologies, procuring military equipment abroad or confining procurement to defense industry at home, and so on.

I suggest the following, somewhat syncretic definition, which will underlie much of what follows in this paper:

"Globalization is the increased speed, frequency, and magnitude of access to national markets by non-national competitors."

In defining globalization this way, I intend it to encompass *all* markets: social, cultural, and recreational markets, including markets for intellectual property, literature, film, media, music, and sports, as well as those for merchandise and commercial services.

3. Measurement Issues and Applications

The preceding definition implies several tendencies in global and national markets, and the conditions we should expect to find or to impend as globalization proceeds. These conditions should, in turn, affect the identification and design of appropriate indicators or metrics for globalization.

First, and most obviously, this definition implies that global markets have become and are becoming more integrated.

Second, increased access to national markets by non-national competitors suggests that disparities across countries in prices, wages, and real interest rates (after allowing for the costs of hedging against exchange-rate risks), should decrease.

Third, with the decline in price gaps among countries, price correlations between markets should increase, and divergences of output patterns across markets should rise due to enhanced opportunities for specialization and the effect of comparative advantage.

Fourth, differences between savings rates and investment rates *within countries* should increase (because investment rates will be less dependent on savings rates than has been true in the past).

Typically, measurement of globalization has focused on the magnitudes of trade transactions and capital flows, based on the premise that the larger these magnitudes, the greater the prevalence or expansion of globalization. Yet, the volume of trade and capital flows are at best imperfect indicators, because of various problems connected with them. For example, trade and capital transactions are subject to wide fluctuations, and the reliability and comparability of the underlying data are often questionable. Trade can be distorted through national policies—such as subsidies to raise exports and tariffs or non-tariff barriers to restrict imports. Consequently, such policies may obscure underlying globalization trends, or may sometimes even make such trends appear stronger than they in fact are.

Notwithstanding these problems, one frequently used indicator of globalization is exports as a proportion of gross domestic (or global) product. Table 1.1 summarizes the long-term trend in global exports as a percent of global product, from 1870 to 1999.

As the figures in Table 1.1 indicate, this ratio as an indicator of globalization isn't monotonic: it moves up and down over time. Indeed, in the 1990s—the period of what has typically been viewed as a relent-

Table 1.1

Exports as a Percentage of GDP, 1870–1999

			Year			
1870	1913	1950	1973	1987	1995	1999
5.9	8.2	5.2	10.3	12.8	17.3	15.0

SOURCES: Kevin H. O'Rourke and Jeffrey G. Williamson, *Globalization and History*, MIT Press, 1999.; Department of Commerce, Bureau of Economic Analysis, 1995, 1999. Data for 1870–1987 cover only merchandise exports for OECD countries; data for 1995–1999 are global and cover *all* exports.

less move toward globalization—the ratio fell between 1995 and 1999.

The volume of international capital flows is another useful and relevant, although also imperfect, indicator of globalization. As with trade data, the data on capital flows are also subject to distortions of various sorts; for example, by tax policies, government-subsidized investment guarantees, and other measures designed to promote or impede such flows.

Interestingly, and contrary to some conventional wisdom, O'Rourke and Williamson (1999) have found that foreign capital flows relative to domestic savings were considerably larger at the start of the 20th century than at its end! However, whereas capital flows at the turn of the century were overwhelmingly in the form of loans, now they consist mainly of foreign direct investment and, to a lesser extent, of portfolio equity investment. One particular form of current capital flows that was virtually non-existent in bygone periods is foreign direct investment (FDI) associated with transborder mergers and acquisitions (M&A). For example, in 1999, FDI for M&A amounted to $800 billion, representing an increase of almost 50 percent from the prior year.

As noted earlier, we might expect on theoretical grounds that globalization should be associated with widening differences between domestic savings and investment rates as a result of greater integration of global capital markets. Figure 1.1 hows the varying correlations between domestic savings and investment rates from 1872 to 1987. While a lower coefficient (the vertical axis of Figure 1) implies a higher degree of integration of global capital markets, Figure 1 shows—once again contrary to much conventional wisdom—that

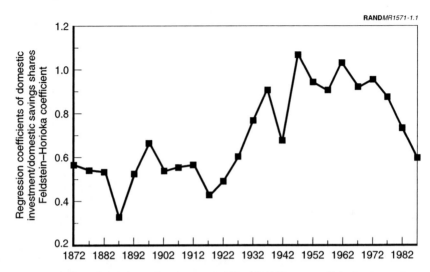

SOURCE: Kevin H. O'Rourke and Jeffrey G. Williamson. *Globalization and History*, MIT Press, 1999; A. M. Taylor, *International Capital Mobility in History: The Saving-Investment Relationship*, National Bureau of Economic Research, Cambridge, Mass., 1996.
    NOTE: Lower correlation implies greater integration of capital markets. Data are for Atlantic economies.

Figure 1.1—Integration of Global Capital Markets: One Indicator

capital markets appear to have been more closely integrated before World War I than they currently are!

In an effort to develop new and improved measures of economic "openness"—an important aspect, if not synonym, of globalization— a recent RAND study devised three additional measures of the relative degree of market access (i.e., economic openness) in five countries: the United States, Germany (as a proxy for the European Union), China, Japan, and South Korea.[2] The three measures are:

---

[2]See Charles Wolf, Jr., Hugh Levaux, and Daochi Tong. *Economic Openness: Many Facets, Many Metrics*. RAND, MR-1072-SRF, Santa Monica, California, 1999.

- a survey questionnaire relating to the relative ease or difficulty of engaging in trade or investment business in the five countries, distributed to the top executives responsible for international operations in 500 multinational corporations;

- a detailed review of legal and administrative documents in each of the countries to assess the extent to which foreign business operations were restricted or prohibited;

- comparisons between the purchasing power parity (so-called "real") value of each country's currency, and its foreign exchange ("nominal") value. (The rationale underlying this measure is that, other things equal, the more "open" an economy, the closer should be the PPP and foreign exchange values of its currency, and conversely.)

The survey was conducted over a five-month period in late 1997 and early 1998 with a response rate of 60 percent. Respondents were asked to respond to a 10-page questionnaire, rating each of the five countries according to a six-point scale (from zero to five) as to the degree of restrictiveness prevailing in each of the countries. Table 1.2 shows the aggregate response means from the survey.

Table 1.3 shows the openness index resulting from the review of legal and administrative documents and regulations referred to above.

Table 1.2

Aggregate Response Means from Business Questionnaire

Country	Openness in Trade	Openness in Investment	Aggregate Openness[a]
United States	1.71	0.97	1.35
European Union	2.43	1.67	2.07
Japan	3.34	2.86	3.13
South Korea	3.21	3.42	3.30
China	3.41	3.94	3.64

[a]Aggregate index is based on the aggregate answers to 20 questions in the openness questionnaire: low index values signify less restriction, hence greater economic openness. The aggregate index is an unweighted average of the trade and investment indexes, subject to rounding.

Table 1.3

Aggregate Openness Index Based on Authors' Evaluations of Administrative and Legal Regulations

Country	Trade	Investment	Overall
United States	1.63	0.90	1.27
European Union	2.53	0.77	1.65
Japan	3.40	2.77	3.08
South Korea	3.77	3.00	3.38
China	3.83	3.77	3.80

Finally, Table 1.4 shows the results of the third metric, comparing the normalized differences between the five countries' purchasing power parities and foreign exchange currency values, during the 1991–1995 period.

The results shown in Table 1.4 diverge slightly from the close congruence between the rankings of openness displayed in Tables 1.2 and 1.3. Yet even this slight divergence (i.e., the shift in ranks between Germany and Korea) is readily attributable to two factors: the differing time periods covered in Table 1.4 compared to that in Tables 1.2 and 1.3; and the sharp impact of German reunification costs in the early and middle 1990s on the disparity between PPP and exchange rate values of the deutschmark. In any case, it is evident that the overall economic openness rankings shown in the three tables for the five countries is strikingly similar.[3]

Table 1.4

Normalized Differences Between Purchasing Power Parities (PPP) and Exchange Rates (XRs), 1991–1995 Averages

Country	Average PPP	Average XR	PPP–XR / XR	Openness Ranking
United States	1	1	0	1
Germany (DM/$)	2.14	1.58	0.35	3
Korea (won/$)	526	778	0.32	2
Japan (yen/$)	184	114	0.61	4
China (RMB/$)	1.43	7.0	0.81	5

---

[3]The probability that the rankings of economic openness shown in Tables 2, 3, and 4 for the five countries are random is less than 2 percent.

Although the metrics we have used may be helpful in calibrating globalization, they clearly fall short of providing an adequate measure of the phenomenon. However, if we can assume that these metrics for economic openness correspond more or less closely to the diffusion of globalization, it can be said that globalization has penetrated in descending order to the economies of the U.S. and the EU, with Japan, Korea, and China well below them, but grouped fairly closely to one another, for the time periods covered by the measurements.

4. Concluding Observations: How Much Globalization Is There, and How Much of It Is New?

There is no question that some aspects of globalization are genuinely new. These include developments in information technology, the unabated progress of Moore's Law (doubling of computer chip capacity every 18 months), the connectivity of the internet, e-mail, e-commerce, transborder M&A, and the scale of FDI. Nevertheless, there is a tendency toward exaggeration of the novelty as well as the magnitude of globalization, as a result of situational myopia, media hype, organized protest demonstrations (for example, against the World Trade Organization in Seattle in 1999, and against the American Free Trade Association in Quebec in 2001), and simple forgetfulness. Contrary to conventional beliefs, the data presented above show that trade as a share of GDP has reached higher levels in the past than recently, that correlations between domestic savings and investment rates were lower at intervals in the past than currently, and that globalization in the sense of foreign access to domestic markets still varies widely among countries.

In a notable recent study that tries to place current global trends in historical perspective rather than treating them as unusual, the authors characterized the global economy in 1914, immediately prior to the first World War, as one in which there was:

> "...hardly a village or town anywhere on the globe whose prices were not influenced by distant markets, whose infrastructure was not financed by foreign capital, whose engineering, manufacturing, and even business skills were not imported, whose labor markets

were not influenced by the absence of those who had emigrated or the presence of strangers who had immigrated."[4]

So, while there is much that is new and distinctive about globalization currently, there is also much about the phenomenon that has abundant precedents.

Furthermore, it should (but doesn't) go without saying that globalization now, like its precedents in the past, is not a zero-sum game. Although there are losses and losers, as well as gains and winners, the aggregate of economic gains exceeds that of losses. While low wage labor in developing countries is "exploited" by the increased penetration of foreign business and investment in domestic markets, the process creates benefits and opportunities that the low wage labor would be denied without globalization.

It is also worth noting that the gains and losses, and their corresponding beneficiaries and victims occur within *both* the rich and poor countries. Increased access to national markets by non-national businesses disrupts high-cost, less-efficient enterprises in developed as well as developing countries. Indeed, most of the anti-globalization protest demonstrations that have occurred in recent years have been led by individuals and organizations from rich, developed countries, rather than poor developing ones.

Finally, experience to date suggests that globalization has been accompanied by, if not necessarily causing, increased income inequalities. Typically, average rates of income growth have, in the aggregate, been similar for the rich, poor, and the general population, resulting in widened income disparities (hence, increases in such inequality measures as Gini coefficients in both developed and developing countries). Whether and to what extent strenuous efforts should be made to redress these effects is a critical issue for policymakers—an issue that is likely to result in quite different choices in different countries.[5]

---

[4]Kevin H. O'Rourke, and Jeffrey G. Williamson. *Globalization and History*. Cambridge: MIT Press, 1999.

[5]The choices are likely to be different as well difficult for many reasons. For example, recent econometric studies strongly suggest there is a significant positive relation between income inequality and economic growth, apparently resolving this long-

Postaudit

The analysis and main points seem to me as valid and relevant now as when they were written in 2000.

---

standng controversy among economists. See Kristin J. Forbes. "A Reassessment of the Relationship Between Inequality and Growth." *American Economic Review,* September 2000.

Chapter 2

GLOBALIZATION: LESS THAN MEETS THE EYE

Globalization is becoming obscured as much as illuminated by the rhetoric surrounding it. If we define it as greater access to markets by foreign businesses, then there is considerably less globalization than has been presumed.

Increased access to markets implies that disparities from country to country in prices, wages and real interest rates should decrease substantially. In fact, while some of these disparities have diminished, most have persisted.

With a decline in price gaps among countries, price correlations across markets should increase, and divergences in production should rise due to enhanced opportunities for specialization in each country. But different economies have continued to emulate one another rather than specialize, sometimes contributing to oversupply and gluts in particular markets. Computer chips, steel and shipbuilding provide three recent examples.

Differences between savings rates and investment rates within countries would be expected to increase with globalization because domestic investment would become less dependent on domestic savings. But domestic savings and investment rates continue to be fairly closely correlated within each country, although they have diverged in Japan and the United States.

*Published in **The International Herald Tribune** on August 10, 2001 under the same title.*

One conventional way of measuring globalization is to express global exports as a proportion of the global product. As this proportion rises, the quantity of globalization is presumed to rise similarly. However, from 1995 to 1999, a period often viewed as marked by a relentless surge of globalization, the proportion actually fell from 17.3 percent to 15 percent. This is not supposed to happen if globalization were as pervasive and dominant as has been contended.

Another way of measuring globalization is by the volume of international capital flows. A recent study by the economic historians Kevin O'Rourke and Jeffrey Williamson has shown that foreign capital flows relative to domestic savings were actually larger at the start of the 20th century than at its end.

Some aspects of globalization, especially ones relating to information technology, are genuinely new: the unabated progress of Moore's Law, which says that computer chip capacity will double every 18 months, the connectivity of the Internet, e-mail, e-commerce, trans-border mergers and acquisitions, and the large scale of foreign direct investment.

Still, there is a tendency to exaggerate the novelty as well as the magnitude of globalization, a tendency reflected in the organized and sometimes violent demonstrations against globalization that occurred in Seattle in 1999 and Quebec and Genoa in 2001.

Globalization is not new. Trade as a share of gross domestic product has reached higher levels in the past than recently. Correlations between domestic savings and investment rates were lower at intervals in the past than they are currently. And globalization, in the sense of access by foreign businesses to domestic markets, still varies widely among countries.

According to a recent RAND study, access by foreign businesses to the markets of Japan, China and South Korea continues to be significantly more restricted than access to the markets of the United States and Germany.

Furthermore, it should go without saying that globalization now, as in the past, is not a zero-sum game. Although there are losses and losers, as well as gains and winners, the aggregate of economic gains exceeds that of losses. While low-wage labor in developing countries is exploited by increased penetration of foreign business and by foreign investment in domestic markets, the process creates benefits and opportunities that low-wage workers would be denied without globalization.

Paradoxically, it can be more convincingly argued that globalization has been too little and too limited to realize these potential gains, rather than having been so pervasive and relentless as to overwhelm resistance by those who would be adversely affected.

Postaudit

The essential point remains valid: There are both reality and hype to globalization. But typically, the hype much exceeds the reality.

Chapter 3

FINANCIAL CRISES AND THE CHALLENGE OF
"MORAL HAZARD"

In the innumerable discussions and debates about Asia's financial turmoil, typically dated from the collapse of the Thai baht on July 2, 1997, the standard script includes an acknowledgment of a phenomenon called "moral hazard" (hereafter referred to as MH). Once MH has been acknowledged, the script calls for it thereafter to be passed over lightly, if not entirely ignored, in favor of other explanations and terminology, including such evocative terms as "financial contagion," "herd-like behavior," "speculative currency attacks," and "predatory hedge-fund speculators."

Although MH is familiar in the lexicon of economists, it has a distinctly "other social-science-besides-economics" tonality. The purpose of this note is to prod other social scientists to provide some insight concerning a phenomenon of central importance, both as a contributing cause and aggravated consequence, of Asia's financial turmoil, its repercussions in Russia, Brazil, Japan, and the United States, and its implications for the recurrence of financial crises in the future.

"Moral hazard" is a disposition on the part of individuals or organizations to engage in riskier behavior, than they otherwise would, because of a tacit assumption that someone else will bear part or all of the costs and consequences if the incurred risk turns out badly. Similarly, but somewhat more formally, MH is defined in the economics

---

*A slightly edited version was published in **Society**, July/August 1999, under the same title.*

literature as: "actions by economic agents in maximizing their own utility to the detriment of others in situations where they do not bear the full consequences . . . of their actions."[1]

The concept, but not the term, is evident in Adam Smith's *Wealth of Nations*, but the term's origin itself is obscure. One can think of other terms that would be at least equally descriptive of the phenomenon without invoking the "moral" ingredient—for example, "conflicted interests," or "mixed incentives." Smith, of course, was himself a professor of *Moral* Philosophy.

I conjecture that derivation of the term MH may owe more to Immanuel Kant, a contemporary of Smith's, than to Smith. Kant's moral imperative asserts that a moral action is one that provides a just and fair precept for the actions of others—a broad and general statement of the golden rule. With this imperative as a standard, the mixed incentives prevailing when responsibility for actions is divorced from responsibility for consequences presents a *hazard* to moral behavior.

MH is certainly not unique in the financial domain. Indeed, it occurs in many aspects and stages of quotidian life. For example, a child may be more disposed to get into one or another kind of trouble because of a belief that her parents will get her out of it; an adolescent may occasionally overspend from his allowance because of prior experience that his parents, perhaps contrary to their expressions of intent, will bridge the gap.

The phenomenon of MH is also pervasively associated with insurance policies, and the behavioral effects they may have. For example, automobile liability insurance may in some cases conduce to less careful driving, and fire insurance on a home perhaps reduces incentives to substitute less flammable for flammable materials, such as tile roofing in place of wood shingles. And even health insurance may sometimes result in excessive utilization of health care services, or in avoiding preventive care, or deferring changes in life-style that would reduce the need for health care.

However, there are at least two important differences between some of these insurance transactions and the MH phenomenon in the fi-

---

[1] *The New Palgrave: A Dictionary of Economics*, Vol. 3, 1987, p. 547.

nancial context. First, in the case of insurance-induced MH, the premiums paid for policies represent a cost paid by the insured that is not directly matched in the case of IMF-bailout provisions to rescue insolvent or illiquid debtors, as in the Mexican financial crisis of 1994, and the Asian crisis since 1997. Second, it is frequently, though not uniformly, the case in insurance transactions that premiums are based on performance and experience, so that the effect of MH on the behavior of insured parties may raise their subsequent premiums costs if indeed the frequency of their requesting insurance claims rises above actuarial calculations.

This is not to say that MH was the principal cause of the Asian financial crisis and its repercussions. However, it is reasonable to suggest that MH operated as a prominent part of the circumstances encouraging risky and overoptimistic behaviors by lenders, borrowers, and other economic actors, directly leading to the Asian financial troubles. These imprudent behaviors included the following components:

1. for individual, corporate, and sovereign borrowers, motivation toward excessive short-term borrowing derived from interest-rate arbitraging between *low* rate hard-currency loans and high interest rate charges on own-currency relending for domestic real estate or other investment;

2. for many money-center banks in Europe, Japan, and the United States, motivation toward excessive lending resulted from a desire to boost their volume and turnover, and hence profits, because of the low costs to the lenders of raising funds domestically, and

3. overvalued exchange rates in the borrowers' countries due to currencies pegged to the dollar at rates that were sustainable only as long as there was a continued inflow of short-term funds from abroad.

It is doubtless that the principal actors engaging in these behaviors were keenly aware of the prior and partly similar predicament of Mexico three years earlier, which was salvaged by a large inflow of bailout funds from the United States and the IMF. So, MH was pervasively operative—that is, a belief that if these behaviors were to run amiss, some type of cushion would be provided by multilateral or bilateral sources. Now that the IMF's capital has been replenished from new subscriptions by the United States to its funding base and prospectively by other countries, and with the Asian Development Bank as another source of "last resort," bailout funding, the prospect is that the MH phenomenon will be reinforced, with baleful consequences in the future.

What sorts of remedies, or at least palliatives, can be devised to offset the operation of moral-hazard behaviors? In the realm of public policy, at least two sorts of remedies may be envisaged. One possible remedy is to allow the financial markets' own homeostasis processes to operate. For example, creditor institutions collectively would bear the responsibility for deciding whether to incur an actual default on debt owed to them, or to organize and share in providing roll-over financing subject to conditions levied on the debtors by the creditor consortium, rather than by governmental bodies.

Another policy course might be to consider the suggestion made by George Soros to set up a multilateral International Credit Insurance Corporation to provide loan guarantees for emerging-market borrowing. Soros's proposal, presented in his recent book *The Crisis of Global Capitalism*, would involve funding the ICIC through the Group of Seven (G-7) and IMF—hence, by the taxpayers of the G-7 countries. An alternative, as well as an improvement, upon this scheme would be to have the corporate financial community self-fund the ICIC through premium charges that might conceivably be performance-based. A performance-based premium schedule would ease, if not fully resolve, the MH problem because unnecessarily risky behavior would, over time, be penalized by charging a higher premium for wayward members of the insurance pool.

From an academic and analytic point of view, the moral hazard issue provides a challenge to the social science community—one that is not confined to economics and economists, whose treatment of the problem has been inconclusive, as well as controversial. As examples of the unresolved controversy, note the following assertions by economists concerned with the Asian financial crisis:

> "There is little, if any, dispute about whether the IMF assistance packages create moral-hazard incentives that could increase the likelihood and severity of financial crises. The unresolved issue is

the extent to which susceptible parties have acted on the incentives."[2]

By way of contrast, another economist opines:

> "The. . . 'moral-hazard' critique . . . is unrealistic . . . the suffering that a country in crisis endures is already so severe that risk-prone parties quickly learn their lesson without lectures about moral-hazard from well-meaning economists."[3]

And finally, George Soros avers that:

> "The IMF is part of the problem, not the solution."[4]

Perhaps other social scientists besides economists can help to illuminate the concept of MH, and suggest remedies for its perverse effects.

Postaudit

Moral hazard remains a serious and pervasive problem to which too little attention is devoted in both academic and policy circles.

---

[2]James Barth, Dan Bumbaugh, Lalita Ramesh, and Glenn Yago. "The East Asian Banking Crisis." *Jobs and Capital*, Summer/Fall 1998, p. 35.

[3]David Hale. "The IMF, Now More Than Ever." *Foreign Affairs*, November/December 1998, p.10.

[4]George Soros. *The Crisis of Global Capitalism*. Public Affairs Press, 1998, p. 148.

Chapter 4

THE MORNING AFTER

In the past two years, major financial quakes have struck three geo-graphically non-contiguous areas: East Asia in July 1997, Russia in August 1998, and Brazil in January 1999. If the sharp jolts in these economies were converted to seismographic readings, they would register at least 6.5 on the Richter scale, about the same as the Los Angeles earthquake in 1994.

In the Asian "crisis" countries—Thailand, Korea, Indonesia, and Malaysia—asset values plummeted by about 75 percent due to the combined effects of currency depreciations and deflated property and equity markets. Averaging over these countries, an asset worth $100 in June 1997 was worth only $25 a year later. In Russia and Brazil, the corresponding asset deflations were more than 70 per-centand 50 percent, respectively. Assets worth $100 before the Russian and Brazilian crashes, were, respectively, worth only about $28 and $50 afterwards.

To place these tectonic crunches in another context, it's worth recall-ing that, in the U.S. financial crises of 1929–1932, 1962, and 1987, the S&P index fell by 87 percent, 28 percent, and 34 percent, respectively.

Explanations for these jolts as well as prescriptions for mitigating them in the future fall into two camps. One ascribes principal blame

---

*A slightly edited version was published in **The Wall Street Journal** on March 2, 1999 under the same title.*

to the miscarriages of "untrammeled" markets that inevitably result in "irrational exuberance," financial "bubbles," "contagion," and "overshooting." Protagonists,who might be labeled the "pro-intervention architects," include George Soros, Eisuke Sakakibara, Mohamad Mahathir, Paul Krugman, and Stanley Fischer. They typically emphasize the errant behavior of unregulated capital markets, speculators, and hedge funds, and prescribe various types of new regulatory interventions applied especially to capital flows, as well as a new "international financial architecture" intended to deter future international financial crises, or to alleviate them if they occur. The IMF's new Contingent Credit Line facility is the first major edifice of this financial architecture. Backed by a $90 billion replenishment of IMF resources, the CCL is intended to provide preventive loans to *potentially* vulnerable economies in order to forestall future financial crises.

The second camp, which might be called the "anti-intervention skeptics," contends that financial crises in Asia, Russia, and Brazil were instead due to *departures* from the operation of free markets. Adherents include Milton Friedman, George Schultz, Alan Meltzer, Andrei Illarionov, and Marvin Krause. In Asia, for example, this camp contends that the financial meltdown, beginning with the collapse of the Thai baht in July 1997 and then rapidly extending to the other crisis countries in Asia, was in fact nurtured by *non-market* interventions and institutions (e.g., governments and multilateral agencies) that could be expected to come to the rescue if seriously adverse consequences ensued.

Hence, such actions as short-term borrowing (and lending) could be allowed to escalate, and interest-rate arbitraging could be promoted with what was thought to be minimal downstream risk. The result was pervasive encouragement of "moral hazard": the usual precepts of "due diligence" were ignored in favor of what might be characterized as "undue negligence." In the workings of "crony" or preferential capitalism in Asia, resources were not allocated according to fair assessments of market risk and realistic expectations of profit and loss, but according to the preferential status of particular sectors, firms, and individuals. The tacit assumption underlying these distortions reflected the prevalence of moral hazards: if seriously adverse consequences occurred, someone else would handle them.

Russia and Brazil displayed several variations on these themes. In Russia, the state's centrally-owned assets were distributed to the emerging "oligarchs" through government fiat, insider dealing, and outright fraud, rather than through open, competitive bidding. The ensuing massive flight of capital from Russia, lubricated by IMF bailout funding, depreciated the ruble by more than 60 percent, and sharply depressed stock market capital values.

Brazil's departures from the market regimen included government pegging of the real at rates made increasingly unrealistic by large and mounting budget deficits. As a consequence, shorting the real and subsequent large-scale capital flight occurred, along with sharp depreciation of the currency—all of these representing predictable market responses to anti-market policies.

Instead of a "new financial architecture," the anti-intervention skeptics concentrate on remedial measures designed to improve the functioning of markets, and to increase rather than diminish reliance on market forces and discipline. The skeptics are averse to the architectural proposals of the activists, professing worries that these remedies will have iatrogenic consequences: the side-effects will be worse than the symptoms they are supposed to relieve. For example, the IMF's CCL, although intended to forestall future financial crises, may instead engender them. The moral hazards created by the CCL will induce its prospective beneficiaries to "game" the credit line to obtain subsidized funding that existing capital markets would not provide, or would only provide at much higher rates.

At a more specific and operational level, the skeptics propose measures that would reinforce, rather than replace, market mechanisms. For example, one remedy would simply allow the homeostatic processes of market mechanisms to operate in the event of financial crises. Creditor institutions would bear *collective* responsibility for deciding whether to incur an actual default on debt owed to them, or instead to organize and share in providing roll-over financing subject to conditions levied on the debtors by the creditor consortium, rather than by governmental bodies. Free-rider temptations within the consortium could be avoided, or at least mitigated, by granting the consortium temporary exemption from antitrust liability, and allowing the consortium to develop its own means of maintaining compliance within the group.

Another device might be to adopt, while modifying, a suggestion made by one of the activists, George Soros, to set up a multilateral "International Credit Insurance Corporation," to provide loan guarantees for emerging-market borrowing. The crucial modification, as well as improvement, in the original proposal would be to have the corporate financial community self-fund this insurance corporation through premium charges that would be performance-based. Such a premium schedule would ease, if not fully resolve, the moral hazard problem: risky behavior would, over time, be penalized by charging a higher premium for loss-prone buyers of the loan guarantees.

There is some evidence that hedge funds, rather than precipitating financial turmoil in the three afflicted regions, actually lost money from it (especially in Russia, Hong Kong, and Malaysia). Nevertheless, some of the market-oriented skeptics would favor *ex ante* disclosure by hedge funds of the extent and sources of their leverage, in the interest of increasing the information available to shareholders of the leveragees.

In the aftermath of the three financial crises of the past two years, it seems clear that where the particular impacted countries have instituted market-oriented policies and institutions, or at least have begun to do so, distinct signs of progress and incipient recovery have ensued. By the second quarter of 1999, Korea and Thailand have turned the corner. Their respective GDP growth is slightly positive in the case of Korea, and much less negative in Thailand than in the prior year. By the fourth quarter of 1999 both countries will probably experience positive growth rates. In both countries, foreign direct investment has resumed—in Korea, FDI increased nearly threefold to more than $2 billion in the first quarter of 1999, compared to the first quarter of 1998. Foreign exchange reserves have increased—slightly in Thailand and substantially to $59 billion in Korea, and Korea's international credit rating has been significantly upgraded by Moody's and Standard and Poor's. In Brazil, where deficit spending has been restrained and the crawling currency peg has been removed, the real has recovered about half of its 1998 value, and foreign exchange reserves have increased by more than threefold.

Although neither Korea, Thailand, nor Brazil is out of the woods, their progress contrasts sharply with its absence in other countries that have not pursued market-oriented policies, notably, Russia, Indonesia, and Malaysia, which continue to experience significantly negative rates of GDP growth, weakened currencies (in Malaysia temporarily buoyed by capital controls), and depressed asset values. The ruble remains at about a quarter of its prior year's value, and its meager foreign exchange reserves have been further depleted. In both Indonesia and Malaysia, while there has been some recovery of currency and asset values, political rather than economic factors predominantly account for the economic quagmire that still engulfs them. Unless and until political stability and a more favorable and predictable policy environment is created, the outlook for Indonesia and Malaysia will remain dim.

In sum, the countries showing strongest signs of recovery from the financial crisis of the past two years are reducing their penchant for interventionist solutions and avoiding the perils of a possibly new financial architecture. More freedom, rather than more intervention, is the path to economic recovery and sustained growth. But so long as the interventionists retain the upper hand in the councils of Western governments and multilateral organizations, the international economy will be prone to financial as well as moral hazards.

Postaudit

The principal error in this assessment is my bearish call on Russia, which has performed better than I expected.

Chapter 5

FINANCIAL FLU ISN'T CONTAGIOUS

Like the dog that didn't bark in the classic Sherlock Holmes story, one of the most significant, as well as neglected, facets of the financial turmoil afflicting the international economy since mid-1997 is what did *not* happen. What did not happen is the global deflation and recession, or anything approaching this dismal prognosis by such occasionally credible sources as *The Economist*, George Soros, Paul Krugman, and others in the past year. In fact, economies producing more than 80 percent of the global product have adjusted with reasonable speed and effectiveness. Nor has the process of their adjustment significantly affected their prior economic performance, whether it had been relatively bad (e.g., Japan), relatively good (e.g., the United States), or something in between (e.g., the European Union).

To be sure, the collapse of currencies and asset markets in Southeast Asia and Korea in 1997, followed in mid-1998 by the plummeting of the Russian ruble, and in 1999 by the still precariously depreciating real in Brazil, have inflicted severely adverse shocks to these economies. And these shocks have undeniably had repercussions elsewhere. Imports and exports by the Asian countries have sharply declined, painfully depressing Asian living standards and GDPs. Correspondingly, exports to Asia from the United States, Europe, and Japan have also declined, and Japan's new investments in Asia have been shut down or curtailed. Foreign capital exited from much of

---

A slightly edited version was published in **The Wall Street Journal** *on March 2, 1999 under the same title.*

Asia, from Russia, and latterly from Brazil. In the Russian case, capital flight followed and reflected the previous flight of indigenous capital engineered by Russia's so-called "oligarchs." In Brazil, capital flight has reflected the government's equivocal policies for controlling and reversing the economy's huge accumulation of both public and private debt.

Nevertheless, the repercussions from the financial turmoil in Asia, Russia, and Brazil have been modest. They have not had major adverse impacts on the performance of most of the global economy. In fact, the international economy has been more robust and resilient than would be inferred from most prior as well as current commentaries.

The U.S. economy has continued to perform creditably, experiencing both limited harm as well as limited benefits from the financial turmoil elsewhere: limited harm in the form of reduced exports to Asia (by 13 percent between 1997 and 1998), limited benefits through the damping effects of increased imports from Asia (by 4 percent between 1997 and 1998), on latent inflationary pressures in the U.S. economy.[1]

The European Union's GDP growth rate, about 2.7 percent in 1998, has been at or above that of recent prior years, notwithstanding the financial turmoil elsewhere, while leaving virtually unchanged the EU's staggering unemployment rate of nearly 11 percent.

Japan's economy has continued to stagnate, experiencing negative growth and rising unemployment. Its lagging performance has been accompanied by a still growing current account surplus, resulting from the economy's deeply ingrained mercantilist policies favoring exports and inhibiting imports.

In both Europe and Japan, admittedly serious economic problems— high unemployment in Europe, negative GDP growth and rising unemployment in Japan—are fundamentally structural and institutional, rather than cyclical in nature. Both the causes of these problems, and remedies for them, are unrelated to and largely unaffected by the financial turmoil in Asia, Russia, and Brazil.

---

[1] Exports and imports based on data for the first 11 months of 1997 and 1998.

The same point applies to most of the developing world, as well. Thus, the Chinese economy has maintained significant growth (even if the officially reported 7.8 percent rate in 1998 may be overstated), while still beset by serious problems in its costly and subsidized state enterprises and its vulnerable domestic banking institutions. No less than in Japan and Europe, China's economic problems are quite independent of the financial difficulties elsewhere in Asia, Russia and Brazil, although surely these problems are not eased by the financial turmoil elsewhere.

India, while realizing at best only modest progress in its efforts to liberalize the economy and reduce its bureaucratic shackles, continues to grow at a creditable annual rate between 4 and 5 percent. Once again, quickening the pace of reform in India depends on factors quite unrelated to the financial troubles encountered in Asia, Russia, and Brazil.

Despite the alarmist emanations from Davos and parts of the Washington Beltway (especially in the vicinity of the International Monetary Fund and the World Bank Headquarters), there is and should be a growing recognition that the acute economic setbacks in Asia, Russia, and Brazil, have been largely due to their defective economic policies rather than to the phenomena of "contagion" from one country to another, or "herd behavior" on the part of foreign investors. (Indeed, to the extent that "contagion" has occurred, it can be attributed as much to the hoped-for balm of external bailout funds, as to the activities of speculators and foreign hedge-fund managers.)

In Asia, these defective policies took the form of huge, often concealed short-term debt and unrealistically pegged exchange rates—policies that were, in considerable measure, abetted by the implicit belief of both lenders and borrowers that succor would be forthcoming from foreign governments or/and multilateral agencies if things went sour.

In Russia, the defective policies took the form of massive fraud and indigenously manipulated capital exports through underinvoicing of product exports and overinvoicing of product imports.

And in Brazil, the culpable policies were reflected by unrestrained fiscal deficits, excessive public and private debt, and an unrealistic and unsustainable exchange rate.

It is indeed noteworthy that if and as such defective policies are replaced by manifestly sensible ones—as Korea and Thailand have proceeded to do in the past year—economic prospects improve dramatically. For example, in Korea, negative GDP growth of about 7 percent in 1998 shows promise of being replaced by 1 or 2 percent positive growth in 1999.

In sum, the robustness and resilience of the international economy and its capacity to absorb unwelcome financial shocks have been drastically underestimated, if not misrepresented, in governmental, as well as academic, circles, and certainly in the multilateral agencies. Whether and how much the activities, subventions, and policy advice of the IMF have contributed to or detracted from this capacity is a matter of legitimate debate. At least the resilience that has been evident in the face of the financial shocks of the past 20 months warrants skepticism as to whether the creation of a "new international financial architecture"—which would inevitably encompass expanded resources and authority for the IMF and the World Bank—is warranted. Imposition of such a construct would be as likely to make the global economy more prone to financial volatility and shocks, as to enhance its capacity for absorbing them.

Postaudit

I plainly did not anticipate the U.S. recession in 2001 and its global repercussions, although the emphasis placed in Chapter 5 on national economic policies, rather than the effects of foreign economic events, is still valid.

Chapter 6

HISTORY HASN'T ENDED: THE STRUGGLE BETWEEN
MARKETS AND GOVERNMENTS RESUMES

In 1992, Francis Fukuyama offered the optimistic forecast that the "end of history" was impending. His thesis was that the collapse of Soviet communism and the pervasive and demonstrated failures of centrally-planned, command economies had led to universal acceptance of market-based, capitalist democracies. So, he contended, the Manichean struggle between them, which dominated the history of the twentieth century, was at an end.

Fukuyama's forecast was premature.

Once again, the old refrains about the shortcomings of markets and "the crisis of global capitalism" (to use the title of George Soros's new book) are being sung by a politically-diverse choir, including Mohamad Mahathir in Malaysia, Yevgeny Primakov in Russia, Oskar LaFontaine in Germany, and Soros. The resumption of history's old refrains has been spurred by a series of financial crises in international markets: Asia's financial turmoil since July 1997, Russia's default in August 1998 on $15 billion of dollar-denominated debt, and the current pressure of capital flight on Brazil's debt-ridden, but otherwise promising, economy.

With these events in mind, critics have joined in attacking the miscarriages of "untrammeled" markets as the principal cause of international financial turmoil. While this is their common ground,

---

*A slightly edited version was published in **The Los Angeles Times** on January 10, 1999 under the title "Markets Run Into Old Foe."*

thereafter the critics diverge in their diagnoses and the policies they recommend for setting things right to compensate for the market's failures.

Thus, Mahathir holds global hedge funds responsible for Malaysia's plight (although the evidence suggests that in fact the principal hedge funds lost rather than made money as a result of the sharp depreciation in the Malaysian ringgit). Given this mistaken premise, Mahathir has moved to isolate and insulate Malaysia from international capital markets by governmental screening and control of capital movements into and out of Malaysia.

Primakov and his first deputy prime minister, Yuri Maslyukov, former head of the Soviet State Planning Agency, propose to remedy Russia's economic deterioration by selective price controls, restrictions on foreign currency transactions, and retaining a large state-enterprise sector in the economy by deferring further privatization and perhaps even reversing some of that which has already occurred.

LaFontaine proposes enlarged government spending programs to raise internal demand and employment, while insulating German and European Union markets from import competition and international financial volatility.

And Soros proposes setting up an International Credit Insurance Corporation, to be financed by the G-7 governments (hence by their taxpayers), to protect national economies, corporate borrowers, foreign lenders, public investors, and hedge funds like his own, from the excessive volatility of short-term capital flows, interest rates, and exchange rates.

These arguments and prescriptions are more reflective of the predilections of their protagonists rather than the imperfections of market-based systems.

First, the "untrammeled" free markets targeted by these criticisms in fact don't exist, nor does the canonical free market system (what Soros calls "market fundamentalism") presume that effective markets function without trammels. For markets to operate effectively, clear and explicit "rules of the game" are essential. These include protection of property rights, legally-binding and enforced contracts, established and reliable modes of resolving disputes, and free and open competition among producers, consumers, lenders, borrowers, and investors. Absent these essential rules of the game—that is, "trammels"—markets will predictably malfunction. On the other hand, if and when these rules are in place as realities, rather than façades, Fukuyama's original hypothesis, that the market system dominates alternatives to it, is demonstrable.

Second, concerning the Asian financial turmoil and its contagion effects, the principal burden is not properly assigned to the operation of free markets. Instead, the burden lies mainly in departures from free markets—for example, promotion and provision of excessive amounts of short-term lending and borrowing, and protracted support for overvalued and pegged exchange rates underwritten by a tacit non-market assumption that governments or multilateral aid agencies would intervene if circumstances turned sour and recourse to a non-market bailout were required.

"Crony capitalism" in Asia has inherently relied on non-market, personalistic, and governmental backing, rather than on market-based allocative processes. This misplaced reliance is one of the core explanations for Asia's financial crisis.

Third, with regard to Russia's special predicament, once again the onus does not lie in the imperfections of the market mechanism, but in departures from it: specifically, the absence of the legal and other institutional "trammels" required for the functioning of effective markets, the evident perpetration of massive fraud in the privatization of state-owned assets for the benefit of an insider's clique (the so-called "oligarchs"), and the accompanying and ensuing capital flight from the ruble. Underlying, and to a considerable extent contributing to, the Russian debacle has been a neglected facet of the IMF-connected "moral hazard" problem: a presumption by many Russian policymakers that, in light of the bailout packages provided by and through the IMF of some $40 billion for Indonesia, $60 billion for Korea, and lesser amounts for Thailand and the Philippines, Russia should expect much larger subventions from these sources than the niggardly $15–$20 billion that the IMF offered.

To assign responsibility for these anomalies to the vagaries of free market systems is to confuse those systems with aberrations from them.

Although the European Union, reinforced by its impending monetary union and single euro currency, is in a different quadrant from the preceding cases, it too shows distinct signs of veering away from free, open, and competitive markets. Having apparently rediscovered the attractions of an activist Keynesian fiscal policy as a possible remedy for its chronic high unemployment problems, the EU finance ministers have recently agreed on measures to insulate the EU from potential external shocks by restricting outflows of capital and limiting import competition. If Oskar LaFontaine moves from Germany's finance ministry to head the European Commission, these trends are likely to be reinforced. Along this path lies a slower rate of growth in the EU's real GDP and a depreciated value of the euro relative to the U.S. dollar.

Finally, what about the destabilizing effects of large, short-term, speculative capital movements? To be sure, there is a need for greater transparency and timely disclosure to avoid the enormous and excessive leveraging by such ill-fated hedge funds as Long-Term Capital Management. The *leveragees*, as well as the general public, should be aware of what the *leveragers* (such as LTCM) are up to, and the risk exposure thereby created. Nevertheless, on a list of the five or six major contributing factors to the international financial contagion of the past year, the destabilizing effects of large hedge funds, including LTCM, Tiger Management, and Quantum, probably rank seventh or eighth. (As an illustration, when the Malaysian ringgit was deeply declining in August and September 1997, the ten largest hedge funds appear to have been buying into the currency, rather than selling it short.)

Whether some form of controls on large movements of short-term capital is desirable in addition to more timely disclosures of how and how much such funds are leveraged, is both arguable and worth arguing about. On the one hand, some type of control, such as the so-called "Tobin tax" or the Chilean type of capital deposit, may contribute to increased financial stability and reduced currency volatility. On the other hand, controls designed to protect against the contagion of financial volatility may instead generate a contagion of additional controls, thereby predictably leading to corruption, evasion, and favoritism in their application.

However this argument may be resolved—most probably through differing choices and consequences in different countries—the struggle between markets and governments, despite Fukuyama's forecast, is unlikely to terminate. It is more likely to follow a cyclical pattern—sometimes emerging, than submerging, over time. History rarely succumbs to initial attempts to end it.

Postaudit

Hindsight does not seem to me to warrant significant change in these views. Depreciation of the euro has been an accurate forecast, but Russia's improved economic performance was not forecasted.

Chapter 7

THE WTO CONTROVERSY: EXAGGERATED FEARS AND UNREALISTIC HOPES

In the five years since it was established in Geneva, the World Trade Organization (WTO) has acquired a prominence based more on the controversy it has aroused than on the influence it has exercised.

Both preceding and since WTO's aborted ministerial meeting in Seattle at the end of November 1999, the controversy has been intense, as well as misconceived and misdirected. The contest for liberalizing the global economy—WTO's ostensible purview— is mainly being played on other turf than that of the WTO.

The controversy has been abetted by several contending sides, each presuming that WTO has powers which in fact it doesn't possess. WTO's opponents, whose efforts were most conspicuously and disruptively evident in Seattle, consist of a diverse set of activists in both developed and less-developed countries. In the developed countries (the so-called "North"), the opponents include labor unions, children's rights advocates, environmentalists, and French farmers—the latter advancing the imaginative argument that, without subsidies and other forms of protection from foreign competition, the quality of Europe's culture, as well as its gastronomy, would suffer. Opposition of labor and environmental groups proceeds from the premise that WTO can and should apply to the less-developed countries (the so-called "South") the same labor and environmental standards which apply in the "North."

---

*A slightly edited version was published in **The Los Angeles Times** on April 9, 2000 under the title "Fears of the WTO's Influence Are Greatly Exaggerated."*

Opposition to WTO in the South is equally diverse. It comprises both recent and long-standing "infant" industries in automotive, machine-building, and other manufactures, whose low productivity and high costs would make them vulnerable to competition from the North if WTO were to insist on removing the various forms of tariff and non-tariff protection they presently enjoy, let alone to impose additional labor and environmental standards that would raise costs and further impair the South's competitive position.

So, in both rich and poor countries, activist opponents are spurred by acute fears that WTO will accelerate the opening of global markets to the detriment of the interests the activists represent.

On the other side of the controversy are WTO's supporters—notably many multinational business, high-technology, and financial enterprises—who view WTO as a vital means of furthering "globalization." Their advocacy is based on hopes that WTO will be able and willing to accelerate economic liberalization by removal or reduction of barriers to freely competitive markets for goods, services, and capital.

Whether impelled by fears or hopes, the contending sides share a view of WTO's power that is belied by its origins, character, record, and prospects.

WTO was created by the Uruguay Round of GATT at the end of GATT's nearly eight years of trade negotiations. It has 135 members (China is the prospective 136th), a secretariat of 500, and an annual budget of 122 million Swiss francs (about $80 million). Its operations conform to the GATT tradition of making decisions by *consensus* among its members, *not by vote*. WTO's three operating entities—the General Council, the Dispute Settlement Body, and the Trade Policy Review Body—include *all* WTO members. Where consensus is not possible, the WTO Agreement allows for the possibility of majority voting, a procedure that will probably be eschewed for the indefinite future because the industrialized countries of the North oppose it. The organization's management structure contrasts (whether for good or ill) with that of the IMF and World Bank. These institutions have executive boards to direct the officers of the IMF and the Bank, with permanent participation by the major industrial countries and *weighted voting* reflecting their dominant financial position. WTO is unlikely to have a comparable structure because the majority membership from the South opposes ceding such control to the North. Although WTO's new Secretary General, Mike Moore, is an experienced and energetic politician (formerly New Zealand's Prime Minister and Trade Minister), what he can do will be severely limited by the constraints inherent in the WTO.

Under these circumstances, it isn't surprising that WTO's efforts to resolve disputes by providing "good offices" and appointing neutral panels of experts have been both dilatory and of little consequence. A case in point is its ineffectual efforts to resolve trade disputes between the United States and the European Union, relating to the EU's banana-import rules and restrictions on imports of hormone-treated beef from the United States. During the past several years, the United States has brought to the WTO charges that these EU restrictions are unfair, unreasonable, and in violation of prior (i.e., GATT) agreements. WTO's review panels found in favor of the United States , thereby triggering appeals by the EU from the panels' decisions, rather than compliance with them. In response, the United States invoked sanctions against the EU under Section 301 of the U.S. Trade Act of 1974. The EU responded with a retaliatory complaint against the United States, charging that Section 301 was illegal because it preempted WTO authority. This charge was rebuffed by another WTO review panel, which judged that use of sanctions did not breach WTO or GATT rules.

It remains to be seen whether the EU will appeal the WTO panel's decision, or instead will comply with the earlier WTO findings. If indeed belated compliance does ensue, it is more likely to have resulted from the U.S. sanctions than from the earlier WTO rulings.

The point isn't that the United States has "won" in its charges against the EU; indeed, there are other instances in which it has "lost." In both cases, the significance of "win" or "loss" is muted by the limited reach of WTO's influence, and the dilatory processes by which it seeks to advance international economic liberalization.

Before too much pessimism is inferred from these indications of what in the European Parliament has been referred to as "liberalization fatigue," it's worth considering another domain where economic liberalization is proceeding with encouraging momentum: *trans-border mergers and acquisitions* (M&A), which is largely (and perhaps fortunately) outside WTO's immediate ambit. Major recent instances of trans-border M&A include Deutsche Bank and Bankers Trust, Daimler and Chrysler, Bertelsmanns and Random House, Renault and Nissan, Ford and Volvo as well as Honda, BP Amoco and Arco, Vodophone-Air Touch and Mannesmann (potentially), and innumerable others. The pace and magnitude represent a remarkable phenomenon with broad implications for international economic liberalization.

Thus, in 1999 global trans-border M&A increased to $798 billion, almost 50 percent above those in 1998. Firms in the United Kingdom were the most acquisitive ($245 billion), followed by the United States ($155 billion), Germany, and France ($93 billion and $92 billion, respectively)—most of the latter two countries' acquisitions occurring within the European Union. In Japan, which hitherto has been relatively impervious to M&A by foreign firms, trans-border M&A rose in 1999 more than threefold to $24 billion, including deals with 65 U.S. firms ($12.1 billion), 25 British firms ($1.6 billion), and 12 French firms ($7.7 billion). Additional trans-border M&A impend in telecommunications, mobile phones, automotive industry, and pharmaceuticals, between firms in the United States, EU, and Japan, on the one hand, and those in India, China, Singapore, and South Korea, on the other.

To be sure, in some instances the incentives motivating trans-border M&A are perversely related to liberalization. Instead, the aim is to gain preferred market access *behind* protected barriers of one form or another, rather than to remove or reduce them. But, in most cases, trans-border M&A depend on, as well as generate, increasing economic openness, the breakup of anticompetitive, restrictive entities and practices (such as the *keiretsu* in Japan), enhanced predictability, increased transparency, and more efficient markets. In general, *realization of the full long-term value of assets acquired by trans-border M&A requires reduced barriers to imports, free access to export markets, and greater openness of domestic capital markets.* Hence, the acquiring and acquired firms are likely to push in these directions. Moreover, under WTO's rules relating to "normal trade relations" among its members, concessions granted by any member—for example, freer access to imports of goods or services—to the firms of another member are supposed to be granted to all. And the ensuing repercussions can also be expected to extend beyond M&A to other forms of direct investment and joint ventures, as well.

The result will advance international economic liberalization, notwithstanding the WTO's limitations and occasional signs of liberalization fatigue.

Postaudit

This assessment of WTO remains valid: The organization will play a useful yet limited role in liberalization of the global economy.

Chapter 8

ECONOMIC FACTS POINT TO A WEAK EURO

The governor of France's Central Bank doesn't have quite the mythic stature of his counterpart in the United States. Nevertheless, Jean-Claude Trichet is one of the most influential and respected figures in Europe's high financial circles. Besides his Bank of France domain, he is also a member of the governing council of the European Central Bank and a prominent candidate to succeed the ECB's present head at the end of his tenure.

So, when Mr. Trichet asserts, as he recently has done, that " . . . the euro is undervalued compared to our [i.e., Europe's] fundamentals," it can be presumed that the assertion reflects a prevalent and perhaps dominant view in those circles.

The euro was established on January 1, 1999 as the common currency for members of the European Monetary Union, which includes all members of the European Union except the United Kingdom, Sweden, Denmark, and Greece. The value off the euro was initially set at 16 percent above the dollar (1 € = $1.16), but thereafter was left to float against the dollar and other currencies.

This initial value was accompanied by a chorus of forecasts from numerous knowledgeable sources—including Nobel prize winner Robert Mundell, Fred Bergsten, Barton Biggs, Roger Kubarych, among many others—that establishment of the euro would reduce the dollar's role as the principal global reserve currency, that the

A slightly edited version was published in **The Wall Street Journal Europe** *on September 6, 2000 under the same title.*

larger size of euroland's collective gross product and trade volume would buttress the euro, and that the result would be a significant weakening of the dollar.

Instead, what has ensued recalls Paul Samuelson's trenchant quip some years ago: "Wall Street indexes predicted nine of the last five recessions." Rather than appreciating, the euro has steadily depreciated against the dollar, settling in recent months at a level about 20 percent below its initial par value (1 € = $.93).

This is the background of Mr. Trichet's assertion.

To assert that a particular market price—in this instance, the euro's dollar price—is "undervalued" is to belie a central tenet of economics: the theory of *efficient markets*. The efficient market theorem, drawing on the work of Friedrich Hayek and Robert Lucas—both Nobel prize winners in economics—postulates that efficient markets incorporate all information available at the time the prices in these markets are set. Consequently, price changes must be attributed to information emerging subsequent to the time any particular price or set of prices was set.

In any event, contradictions to this theory sometimes do occur in practice. Markets may overshoot for a host of institutional or psychological reasons—for example, so-called "herd" behavior, or "contagion" effects, or the effects of arbitrary rules of thumb governing buying and selling operations by large institutional investors. And such overshooting or undervaluations may take time to correct through price movements in the direction presumably indicated by new information—in the case of the euro, new information about the "economic fundamentals" which Mr. Trichet alludes to, although without further specification.

These "fundamentals" presumably are factors affecting the demand for and supply of euros and dollars in international markets. However, the difficulty this presents for Mr. Trichet's contention is that examination of the "fundamentals" does not support the contention that the euro is undervalued.

On the one hand, euroland will probably continue to have a trade and current account surplus (about .6 percent of its gross product), while the United States has a large current account deficit (nearly 4 percent of its gross domestic product). In itself, this would tend to boost the euro's value. But this first of the "fundamentals" is offset by a second: the continuing outflow of direct investment (recall Deutsche Bank/Bankers Trust, DaimlerChrysler, Bertelsmanns/ Random House, Vodaphone/AirTouch, BP/Amoco, etc.), and large-scale portfolio capital from euroland seeking higher-yielding assets in dollarland. And this outflow, of course, tends to strengthen the dollar and weaken the euro.

Among the several other "fundamentals," the balance is still less favorable for the euro. For example, the increased economic growth that is underway in Europe and the slower growth that may impend in the United States will still leave U.S. growth about 1 percent above that of Europe. Also, while labor productivity in the United States is only slightly above that in Europe, total factor productivity—a rough measure of technological advance based on a weighted combination of both labor and capital inputs—is appreciably higher in the United States than in Europe.

Inflation is not an evident problem in either Europe or the United States, thanks to the successful management of monetary policy by the ECB and the Federal Reserve, respectively, and to the current and prospective large budget surpluses in the United States. Germany's recent tax reforms, and especially its planned elimination of capital gains taxes over the next two years, are encouraging signs of a loosening of capital markets in Europe's largest economy. Such measures might be expected to enhance the euro's value if they were not overbalanced by another "fundamental" factor: namely, the expanded regulatory reach of the European Commission in Brussels and its top-level cabinet of 20 power-hungry Commissioners.

Finally, there remains the "fundamental" anomaly of the purchasing power *disparity* between the euro and the dollar: even with a euro valued at 93 U.S. cents, most consumer goods are more expensive in Europe than in the United States.

The bottom line is quite the contrary of the Trichet supposition: when the "economic fundamentals" are examined, they add up to at least as strong a case for an *overvalued* as for an *undervalued* euro. This conclusion also provides some redemption for the efficient markets theorem in practice as well as in theory.

Postaudit

This forecast in 2000 has proved to be right on target. The euro had depreciated another 10 percent by 2002.

Chapter 9

E PLURIBUS INCERTUM UNUM
(FROM MANY AN UNCERTAIN UNION)

Review of Larry Neal and Daniel Barbezat, *The Economics of the European Union and the Economies of Europe*, Oxford University Press, 1998, 396 pp., and Stephen F. Overturf, *Money and European Union*, St. Martin's Press, 1997, 303 pp.

On January 1, 1999, the European Monetary Union (EMU) will be inaugurated. Probably two-thirds of the fifteen members of the European Union (EU) will be included in the EMU's initial membership. Although the Maastricht Treaty of 1992 laid down exacting budgetary and financial criteria for EMU membership (which few of the prospective members will be able to meet without highly creative accounting), the Treaty also provided ample flexibility for admitting to EMU membership countries judged to be "approaching" the requisite financial criteria "at a satisfactory pace." The non-included bystanders among the initial EMU membership are likely to be the United Kingdom (which, despite the fact that it is one of the few EU members whose financial status actually meets the Maastricht criteria, will probably opt out initially), as well as Spain, Portugal, and Greece.

At the center of EMU will be the European Central Bank (ECB), modelled after the German Bundesbank and, like that exemplar, charged with primary responsibility for maintaining noninflationary monetary policy and price stability throughout the EU. The ECB will

*A slightly edited version was published in **The Wall Street Journal** on April 1, 1998 under the title "All for One Currency, One for All."*

be at the helm of the European System of Central Banks (ESCB), which will include the individual central banks of member states. ECB will thus be analogous to the Federal Reserve Board of Governors, while the national central banks will be counterparts of the regional reserve banks in the U.S. Federal Reserve system.

The objectives and possible effects of EMU are numerous, ambitious, and perhaps unrealistic: creation of a strong EU-wide currency, the euro, intended to rival the U.S. dollar as the primary international reserve currency; helping to make the EU an economic powerhouse in the global economy; and leading to formation of a future political and security union for the European community.

All elements in the foregoing scenario are uncertain, but those mentioned in the immediately preceding paragraph are even less likely than those mentioned in the prior ones. Although the EU is one of the world's largest trading regions, over 80 percent of its trade is within the European region. Whether formation of EMU will bring a wider opening of EU trade and capital markets to non-EU trade and investment is doubtful. Unless and until such opening occurs, the role of the euro as an international reserve currency and of the EU as an economic power will be limited.

Money and European Union by Stephen Overturf (St. Martin's Press, 303 pp., $45) and *The Economics of the European Union and the Economies of Europe* by Larry Neal and Daniel Barbezat (Oxford University Press, 416 pp., $60) provide authoritative, balanced, and detailed descriptions and analysis of the institutional and terminological complexities of the European Union, the European Monetary Union, and the EU's complex bureaucracy, procedures, and vocabulary. To help clarify these complexities, Neal and Barbezat provide a valuable glossary of several dozen acronyms that abound in discussions of the EU and the prospective EMU. The authors, all economics professors, cover different though partly overlapping material.

Neal-Barbezat is intended as a text for university courses dealing with the broad subject of European economic integration. Tracing the European Union's history from the Treaty of Rome in 1957 through the Maastricht Treaty of 1992 and the ensuing measures to launch EMU in 1999, the authors show clearly that the drivers have been political no less than economic. Britain's partly-in, partly-out stance has reflected its interest in retaining its "special relationship" with the United States and restraining the growth of the Union's bureaucracy in Brussels. France, on the other hand, is reliant on the bureaucracy's growing power to enhance French influence in the Union as a counterweight to Germany. While some European countries have "opted out" (Norway, Switzerland, and Iceland) of the Union, one (Turkey) has been "locked out."

Overturf's focus is more explicitly on the prospective monetary union, treating the history, process, and institutions of European integration from the standpoint of Europe's evolving monetary system and its movement toward monetary union. Overturf concludes, as have most other writers on the subject, that the strictly economic effects of EMU are likely to be perverse: its costs will probably exceed its benefits. The principal reason for this conclusion is that greater price stability and reduced transaction costs of trade (i.e., the benefits of EMU) will be more than offset by EMU's costs: namely, the adverse economic effects of relinquishing the use of interest rate and exchange rate variations to make adjustments periodically required by the labor immobility and wage rigidity of the European economies.

In the final analysis, the case for EMU is fundamentally political. From Europe's standpoint, or at least the standpoint of key European leaders rather than European publics and electorates, monetary union is believed to be meritorious because it will contribute to European Political Union (EPU). Yet this reasoning may be self-contradictory. Whether EPU lies at the end of the EMU trail will probably depend to a considerable extent on whether EMU has positive or negative economic consequences. If these consequences turn out to be predominately negative, EMU itself may set back, rather than advance, the prospects for Europe's political union.

Postaudit

The skepticism expressed in this review of the European Union's prospects remains warranted. Nevertheless, the EU is a functioning reality, although one whose effectiveness is probably less than its advocates had hoped or expected.

Chapter 10

THE CRISIS OF GEORGE SOROS

Some books evoke as much interest because of their authorship as because of their content. George Soros's new book (*The Crisis of Global Capitalism*, Public Affairs, $26, 284 pages) qualifies on both counts. Soros himself acknowledges that his views "enjoy widespread respect and recognition not because of my philanthropy or philosophy, but on account of my ability to make money in the financial markets... [and my] reputation as a financial wizard."

Soros is the multibillionaire head of Soros Fund Management, which oversees the Quantum Fund. Quantum is putatively one of the world's largest and most nimble hedge funds, a genre whose descriptive label is ironic because its purveyors often court, rather than hedge, risk, if the associated rewards appear attractive. Soros is also the founder of a network of well-endowed "Open Society Foundations" in Eastern Europe, Russia and the United States dedicated to the promotion of more open and democratic societies and politics.

The book (hereafter referred to as *Crisis*) is an unusual amalgam of political philosophy, personal memoir, and dissection of the global capitalistic system. It is also unusual because it presents a virulent assessment of capitalism, its advocates, and its prospects. Soros's assessment employs a harsh and exaggerated rhetoric that recalls Marx, Engels, and Lenin, rather than the bland prose of the financial press or academic texts on comparative economic systems.

A slightly edited version was published in **The Wall Street Journal** *on December 8, 1998 under the title "A Quantum Leap."*

In the realm of political philosophy, to which he devotes nearly half the book, Soros forcefully endorses the goal of "open society," generously acknowledging the debt he owes to Karl Popper, both for the original concept and its classic exposition in *The Open Society and Its Enemies* (Princeton, 1950). Soros tries to enlarge Popper's concept of "Open Society," defining it as "an imperfect society that is always open to improvement." Yet, he actually short-changes Popper by ignoring one of the central precepts of the Open Society—namely, its social mobility and the access to opportunities it affords its members. And, whereas the "enemies" of the Open Society targeted by Popper were totalitarianism in general, and communism and fascism in particular, in Soros's hit list the principal enemies are "market fundamentalists" and the global capitalist system. Indeed, in terms of the gap between their grand intentions and "disappointing outcomes," Soros explicitly places "market fundamentalism" in the same quadrant with communism! And in terms of the "imperialistic tendencies" of the "global capitalist system" to be "hell-bent on expansion" and eventual collapse, Soros contends that the system is "little different from Alexander the great or Attila the Hun"!

In Soros's lexicon, "market fundamentalism" is synonymous with "laissez-faire ideology." It presumes that government intervention in the economy yields negative results, that unregulated markets are perfect markets, and that without the distortions introduced by governments, markets will generate equilibrium between demand and supply, producers and consumers, buyers and sellers, lenders and borrowers.

Soros emphatically disagrees with all of these postulates, even if they are simply formulated as tendencies and probabilities, rather than as steady-state actualities. He asserts that "market fundamentalism came to dominate policy around 1980," which he unmistakably and repeatedly attributes to Ronald Reagan and Margaret Thatcher.

Crisis assigns to market fundamentalism primary responsibility for development of the global capitalist system, a system that Soros asserts is fundamentally flawed. Its flaws include the sharply escalating and asymmetrical "boom/bust cycles" generated by a large unregulated international banking system, and by the huge movements of financial capital from Western financial centers into and out of the "periphery" of Asia, Russia, and Latin America. This boom/bust instability leads to acute "pain" in the poorer periphery regions, a choice by individual countries (for example, Malaysia) to "opt out of the global capitalist system, or simply fall by the wayside" (Indonesia and Russia), and an inability of the international monetary authorities "to hold [the system] together."

These inherent flaws lead Soros to predict the imminent disintegration of the global capitalist system, and to assert that ". . . the global capitalist system will succumb to its own defects." In support of his apocalyptic forecast, Soros recounts his own prominent role in trying to forestall the Russian financial meltdown in August 1998 by proposing the injection of a minimum package of $15 billion of G-7/IMF funds to stabilize the ruble and the Russian stock exchange—a recounting accompanied by more than a hint of *schadenfreude* because Soros's advice was rejected by the IMF and the U.S. Treasury, and, incidentally, his hedge fund experienced major losses!

To delay, if not reverse, his dire prediction of systemic collapse, Soros proposes establishing an International Credit Insurance Corporation to guarantee loans made to periphery countries—such as Korea, Thailand, and Brazil—which otherwise "are doomed to languish in depression for an extended period." Funds for the ICIC would be provided by the G-7 governments, hence by their taxpayers.

Soros's diagnosis of the flaws in "market fundamentalism" and global capitalism displays more flaws than the objects of his criticisms.

The flaws in his arguments include the following:

1. The canonical free market system (i.e., "market fundamentalism") that *Crisis* deplores *requires,* rather than *precludes,* clear and explicit rules of the game to function effectively. These include the rule of law, protection of property rights, legally-binding and enforced contracts, established and reliable modes of dispute resolution, and free and open ("transparent") competition among producers, consumers, lenders, borrowers, and investors. Effective markets are not "untrammeled" markets, as Soros claims, and "market fundamentalists" do not eschew certain "trammels"—instead, they require them!

2.   The "crisis" in international financial markets—triggered by the Asian financial turmoil since July 1997 is not properly assigned, as Soros asserts, to the operation of free markets. Instead, the burden lies mainly in departures from free markets—specifically, in promotion of excessive amounts of short-term lending and borrowing, and protracted support for overvalued, pegged exchange rates, underwritten by a tacit *non-market* assumption that governments and multilateral aid agencies would intervene to protect lenders if circumstances turned sour (an assumption unfortunately validated by subsequent events).

3.   Market "fundamentals" and the "global capitalist system" have an inherent resilience based on feedback and adjustment—what in biological systems is called homeostasis—which Soros largely ignores. To be sure, this resilience can be significantly abetted by prudent public policy measures, such as the Fed's recent and moderate lowering of short-term interest rates.

Scattered throughout Soros's *tour d'horizon* are numerous distracting factual errors. The Chinese currency was devalued in 1994, not 1996 (actually, the yuan *appreciated*, not depreciated, between 1994 and 1996); so it's a mistake to offer, as Soros does, yuan depreciation as a cause of the Asian financial debacle of 1997. Another example: Soros mistakenly contends that social goals "such as providing employment" have taken "second place" in the EU due to international competition, ignoring the effects of a swollen and perverse welfare system in contributing to Europe's high unemployment rates. It is equally erroneous, if not foolish, to proclaim that "the dismantling of the welfare state" is well underway, at a time when welfare expenditures, in Europe especially and in the United States, comprise the dominant share of the respective government budgets. It is also worth noting, contrary to Soros's contention, that the most "fundamental" capitalist system (viz., the United States) is the one in which the "social goal" of low unemployment has lately been farthest advanced.

Finally, Soros's emergency prescription of a publicly- (hence, tax-payer-) funded ICIC is belied by his own insightful analysis of the miscarriages of the IMF, its protection of bank lenders rather than borrowers, its role in aggravating the moral hazard problem, and his own conclusion that the "IMF is part of the problem, not part of the solution." Inevitably, Soros's ICIC would intensify the moral hazard in international financial markets, perversely protecting imprudent behavior while penalizing prudence.

Although Soros advocates humility and the redemptive effects of acknowledging personal "fallibility"—a term that is central to his personal philosophy—he rarely displays either characteristic. In one of his rare professions of humility, Soros concludes by affirming that "All I wanted to do was to stimulate a discussion out of which the appropriate reforms may emerge." At least in this respect, *Crisis* achieves its author's objective.

Postaudit

As this review of George Soros's book suggested in 1998, his forecasts about capitalism's doom were and are flawed. But Soros himself remains an interesting enigma.

Part II

The U.S. Economy and Foreign Policy

Chapter 11

WHETHER AND WHEN TO INTERVENE

The first anniversary of U.S. troop deployments in Kosovo highlights a crucial and controversial question which the eventual presidential debates should, but probably won't, address: Whether and when should the United States intervene to forestall, mitigate, or counter ethnic conflicts and other violations of human rights abroad?

Such interventions span a wide range of operations: peacekeeping (Bosnia over the past five years); peacemaking (Kosovo in the past year); "operations other than war" (Somalia, Haiti, and Rwanda in prior years); and the provision of humanitarian assistance in militarily insecure circumstances (all of the above). In the lexicon of military planners, these operations are collectively referred to as "small scale contingencies" (SSCs), in contrast to operations designed to deter or to meet "major theater wars" (MTWs).

At the end of 1999, the U.S. had 253,000 military forces deployed in foreign countries, of which 46,000 were afloat but ported or regularly refueled abroad, while the remainder was shore-based. Most of these forces are deployed in 11 NATO countries, plus Japan and Korea, reflecting America's alliances and treaty obligations. Nevertheless, it is the smaller deployments growing out of the SSCs—Bosnia and Herzegovina (5,800), Serbia including Kosovo (6,400), Macedonia (1,100), and 13,000 in the Middle East, a legacy of the Gulf War in 1991—that account for a disproportionate share of the stress and fatigue under which the military establishment currently labors.

---

*A slightly edited version was published in **The Los Angeles Times** on November 5, 2000 under the title "To Intervene or Not to Intervene."*

There are numerous reasons for this disproportion. Families are not allowed in the SSC-type deployments, a restriction that coincides with a peak in the percentage of married men and women serving in the armed forces. Repeated and protracted separations have disruptive effects on families and on service morale, which add to the services' difficulties in meeting their retention and recruitment goals in face of the competing pull of strong civil labor markets.

For many years, the U.S. military establishment has been principally sized and configured to deal with MTWs, not SSCs. The main determinant of U.S. force planning has been the goal of meeting two simultaneously-occurring MTWs, in Northeast Asia and the Middle East. It is thus implicitly assumed that, if two MTWs can be effectively dealt with (i.e., a "worst-case" scenario), a sufficient though unspecified number of SSCs can also be managed, because the SSCs constitute "lesser-included" demands for military capabilities.

This is a drastically abbreviated and simplified version of the long-standing and enduring logic of U.S. military planning, a logic that, while occasionally modified at the edges, is imperfectly congruent with America's actual military interventions and deployments in the post–cold war era.

Serious questions arise concerning the actual effectiveness of SSC-type actions and ensuing deployments. Such interventions typically occur in complex political and ethnic circumstances that are neither well-understood nor effectively managed by foreign policymakers, military forces, and cumbersome bureaucracies, however laudable their intentions. The ability of U.S. and other intervention forces to correctly assess these situations, to maneuver effectively in them, and to ameliorate let alone resolve them is both severely limited and beset by uncertainties and perverse consequences. The sobering ambiguities were strikingly portrayed by a cover picture in the London *Economist* last year showing a bereaved and weeping Kosovo woman below a caption that posed the question: "Victim of Kosovo—or NATO?"

Debate over the pros and cons of such interventions reflects two opposed stances. On one side, opponents of interventionism—the so-called "realist" school—argue that U.S. intervention should occur only when "vital national interests" are at stake, quite apart from humanitarian considerations, and whether or not the contemplated actions are multilateral or unilateral. The realist argument contends further that most recent interventions—Somalia, Haiti, Rwanda, Bosnia, and Kosovo—didn't pass this stringent test, although intervention in the Gulf to repel Iraq's invasion of Kuwait ostensibly did.

On the other side, supporters of intervention—the "liberal" or "idealist" school—reply that humanitarian considerations, including the furtherance of ethnic and religious tolerance, protection of human rights, and the advancement of democracy, represent core American values. Hence, tangible support for these values is itself a vital national interest. It can be hoped, if not expected, that exchanges between the presidential candidates before November will address this issue. Were they to do so, one element missing from the standard debate might be usefully added to it.

The Hippocratic oath instructs those pursuing the medical profession: "above all, do no harm." This is too exacting to be fully complied with where military intervention is contemplated, because these situations are ambiguous and complex, and defy precision and certainty. Nevertheless, when U.S. policymakers contemplate intervention they should do so with abundant humility, if not timidity, because of the profoundly uncertain connections between the blunt instruments they can use, and the complex ends they seek.

Perhaps there are ways to hone these instruments so they can be used with greater dexterity and less risk of inflicting inadvertent harm. One way— an adaptation of what once was referred to as the "Nixon Doctrine"—is to equip and train the afflicted side of a local conflict (for example, the Bosnians brutalized by the Serbs), instead of committing intervention forces from outside. A second approach is to earmark a part of U.S. military forces specifically for SSC-type interventions, training and equipping them to maximize their effectiveness in these "lesser" contingencies. Neither of these measures is riskless, but they may still be better than the alternatives.

Even if the Hippocratic oath would remain too exacting to be applied literally, there is a corollary that should be obligatory: Recognize that harm will be an inevitable consequence of intervention, and therefore try to demonstrate convincingly, *before intervention occurs*, that such harm will be substantially less than the desired, although uncertain, improvement that is sought.

From the standpoint of U.S. declaratory policy, a cautionary admonition by Abraham Lincoln is also relevant: "We should not promise what we ought not, lest we be called upon to perform what we cannot."

Postaudit

The terrorist attacks of 9/11 and Operation Enduring Freedom place U.S. intervention in an entirely different context. Still, the cautionary concerns expressed here remain valid.

Chapter 12

TAX CUTS, DEBT REDUCTION, AND "FAIRNESS": WHY TAX REDUCTION IS NO MORE "UNFAIR" THAN DEBT REDUCTION

Critics of the Bush Administration's tax reduction plan fault it on two principal counts: too large, and "unfair" because the resulting benefits accrue disproportionately to high-income earners.

According to the critics, tax cuts should be more selective (that is, "targeted")—hence "fairer"—and smaller, thereby allowing more of the estimated future budget surpluses to be used to pay down the federal government's $3.4 trillion of publicly-held debt over the next 10 years. The implication is that accelerated debt reduction—which would be possible if tax reductions were smaller—would be "fairer" than would the larger, across-the-board cuts in tax rates and tax revenues envisaged by the Bush plan.

On the issue of whether larger tax reductions, or accelerated debt reduction is "fairer," the critics are plainly wrong: the benefits of debt reduction are no less concentrated on high-income earners than are the benefits of tax reduction. The underlying issue of how fairness should be judged is more debatable, more difficult, and probably unresolvable because it is inherently subjective.

To be sure, cutting marginal tax rates by equivalent percentages across the board will disproportionately reduce the dollar tax liabilities of high-income earners. A 5 percent reduction in the marginal

A slightly edited version was published in **The Wall Street Journal** on April 17, 2001 under the title "Tax Fairness Is in the Eye Of the Beholder."

tax liability of a taxpayer whose tax rate is 39 percent reduces tax obligations by much larger *dollar* amounts than does the same 5 percent reduction for a taxpayer whose marginal tax rate is 15 percent because the 39-percent taxpayer typically has more dollars exposed to the higher tax rate.

But the same disproportion arises in the relative dollar benefits that would accrue to high-income earners (hence, high taxpayers), as a result of paying down the federal debt. Reducing federal debt relieves *future* taxpayers of the burden of servicing and redeeming the debt. *Hence, high-income earners—who bear a disproportionate share of this burden through the higher tax rates that they pay—would realize the same disproportionate benefits from this relief as those they would realize from across-the-board tax reduction.*

About 200 years ago, economist David Ricardo made essentially this same point when he analyzed the distributional effects of the comparable, although opposite, choice between incurring government debt *now* to be serviced in the future, or increasing tax revenues now to avoid budget deficits that would necessitate future debt service. Paying down the debt is no less skewed in favor of high-income earners (hence, high taxpayers), than is ratcheting marginal tax rates downward! So, it doesn't make sense to criticize the latter as "unfair" without attaching the same label to the former.

While the issue of tax reduction versus debt reduction can be dealt with and disposed of in economic terms, this is not true of the fairness issue. "Fairness" is complex, multifaceted, and highly subjective. It depends on which among many plausible but conflicting concepts and criteria one adopts for judging, let alone measuring, it.

For example, according to Harvard legal philosopher John Rawls, fairness requires that priority and precedence should be given to providing benefits to the less fortunate (read, "low-income") public before according *any* distributional benefits to the more fortunate (read, "high-income") public. A similar inference follows from the familiar Marxist precept: "from each according to ability, to each according to needs."

Economic theory suggests a very different view of fairness. Here, the touchstone of fairness is productivity. A "fair" distribution of benefits (from wages, or profits, or any distributive share), is one that recognizes the recipient's productivity and rewards it accordingly. Since high taxes paid by high-income earners typically reflect relatively high productivity, so too should the benefits from tax reduction recognize their productivity and reward it accordingly. In this view, it is entirely "fair" that a high share of dollar tax remissions should go to high taxpayers.

This view corresponds closely to what is sometimes referred to as "vertical equity": namely, treating unequally-situated taxpayers (read, high- and low-taxpayers), in appropriately *different* ways (for example, by tax reductions that provide differing amounts of dollar recompense to taxpayers in accord with the differing amounts of taxes they have paid).

Finally, it is worth noting that, when marginal tax rates are reduced by about the same number of percentage points across the board (as proposed by the Bush plan), the *proportional* reduction in the lowest tax bracket is much *larger* than the corresponding reduction in the highest bracket—33 percent and 14 percent, respectively.

This is not to say that *any* distribution of tax cuts is as fair as any other, but rather that there are many reasonable criteria for judging fairness. To argue that the *only* fair distribution of benefits from tax reductions is one which denies high taxpayers an equivalently high share of the benefits resulting from tax reductions is unconvincing.

Whether this argument may nonetheless have appeal on political grounds is a separate question.

Postaudit

The concept of "fairness" is complex and subject to many interpretations. When applied to judging the pros and cons of changing marginal tax rates, it should not be assumed that the easiest interpretation is the most appropriate one.

Chapter 13

FALSE ALARMS ABOUT THE U.S. TRADE DEFICIT

An alarmist consensus is emerging among economic forecasters and commentators that the U.S. trade deficit in 1998 and 1999 will "soar," "surge," and reach "huge levels." Prudent observers should treat this consensus, like others arrived at by economic forecasters, with a healthy degree of skepticism. As an eminent Nobel Prize-winning economist, Paul Samuelson, once noted, "Economists have correctly predicted nine of the last five recessions."

The consensus forecast of a soaring U.S. trade deficit is very likely to be wrong once again. Moreover, even if the forecast were closer to the mark than it is likely to be, its limited significance would not warrant the alarm that commentators are sounding. As Walter Wriston and I wrote in these pages some months ago (June 19, 1997), the trade deficit is one of the least significant indicators of the economy's vitality and health.

In any event, the consensus view that the trade deficit—to be more precise, the current account deficit, which measures the excess of payments for imports of goods and services (including capital services), over earnings from the corresponding exports—will soar is based on several seemingly persuasive arguments.

First, U.S. markets will experience a "flood" of cheap exports from Asia in the wake of the deep depreciation of many of the Asian currencies by more than 50 per cent, and of the Japanese yen by more

---

*A slightly edited version was published in **The Wall Street Journal** on March 5, 1998 under the title "False Alarms on the Trade Deficit."*

than 25 per cent. Second, so the argument runs, U.S. exports to Asia including Japan, which represented about 25 per cent of global U.S. exports, will decline sharply for a number of reasons stemming from Asia's financial turmoil: the severe setback to economic growth in Korea and Southeast Asia; continued stagnation in Japan; the appreciated U.S. dollar, which makes U.S. exports more expensive to foreign buyers; the depleted holdings of dollar assets in the Asian countries (apart from Japan, China, Hong Kong, and Taiwan); and the austerity imposed on the Asian countries by the IMF-led bailout "conditionalities."

The conclusion drawn by the consensus view is that the current account deficit, which was about $114 billion in 1997, approximately 1.4 per cent of the U.S. GDP, will jump to between $150 and $165 billion in 1998, representing perhaps 1.9 per cent of 1998 GDP.

These arguments are more impressive on first glance than on second thought. Counters to them are less obvious, but at least equally strong.

While exports to the United States from Asia will increase as a result of the price advantage conferred on Asian exporters—at least in the short run—by the depreciation of their currencies, it is by no means clear that the volume of these exports will increase by more than the decrease in their dollar prices. Unless their export volume increases by more than their export prices fall, the resulting dollar value of these exports will drop. For example, if the dollar prices of Asia's exports to the United States of goods and services—ranging from agricultural products and toys to apparel, from consumer electronics and computers to cars—decline by, say, 20 per cent in 1998 compared to 1997, the volume of these exports bought by the United States will have to rise by more than 20 per cent for the U.S. trade deficit to be affected adversely.

Furthermore, exports to the United States depend not only on export prices, but on U.S. economic growth. That growth, which was more than 3.5 percent in 1997, is likely to be somewhat less than 3 percent in 1998. So, the boost provided by U.S. economic growth to U.S. imports from Asia, as well as from the rest of the world, will probably abate from what it was in 1997.

To be sure, exports from the United States are likely to fare poorly in most Asian markets in 1998. While the "conditionalities" of the IMF bailout packages point toward more openness of the beleaguered Asian economies, the slowdown in their economic growth, as well as their painfully straitened financial circumstances—even if eased somewhat by the IMF injection of liquidity—will erode their capacity to import from the United States and the rest of the world. On the other hand, resurgent growth in Latin America may provide at least a partial offset to reduced export markets in Asia. And in Japan, which does not suffer from the same financial stringencies as the Korean and Southeast Asian economies, there may be opportunities for U.S. exports to rise if Japan's fiscal stimulus measures have an effect, and if some easing occurs in Japan's neo-mercantilist protection of its domestic markets.

Finally, the consensus alarmism about the impending trade deficit ignores a crucial macroeconomic consideration. The U.S. current account deficit must exactly equal the shortfall in gross savings compared to gross investment in the American economy. The common sense of this equation is simply this: when the resources absorbed by domestic investment exceed those provided by domestic savings, the difference must be imported from abroad. Several major trends in the economy augur at least a modest increase in U.S. savings rates. One such trend is the potential federal budget surplus, foreshadowed by President Clinton's State of the Union message at $10 billion for 1998. This could be still larger if something like $30–$40 billion of new spending for education, child care, and other discretionary programs were to be curtailed. It is also true, that the budget surplus envisaged by the president may turn out to be smaller for many reasons—for example, tax revenues may be less than estimated if economic growth slows down, the yield from the expected tobacco settlement may be less than anticipated, and so on. However, what is nearly certain is that the budget deficit of the past year and prior ones will shrink, whether or not a surplus is actually realized. Hence public *dis*saving will decrease, and U.S. gross savings will rise.

A second trend pointing in the same direction is the possible increase in the personal and household savings rates of the baby-boomers, triggered by their increased attention to and worries about the solvency of Social Security—quite apart from whether in fact these worries are justified.

While there are thus convincing reasons for expecting at least a slight boost in U.S. savings rates, there don't appear to be consequential reasons for expecting a commensurate rise in U.S. investment. Somewhat slower economic growth in 1998 compared to 1997 probably foreshadows at most a constant, and perhaps lower, level of domestic investment.

So gross savings are likely to rise, while investment is not, and the current account deficit in the final analysis depends on the imbalance between investment and savings. Hence, there are compelling reasons for inferring that the current account deficit of $114 billion in 1997 won't rise by much, if at all, in 1998.

Once again, the consensus view—in this case of an exploding current account deficit—is likely to be a false alarm, like the predictions of past recessions that didn't happen.

Postaudit

While the analysis reads well, its forecast was plainly wrong, and by a wide margin. The U.S. current account deficit has steadily increased since 1997.

Chapter 14

TWO DEFICITS THAT JUST DON'T MATTER
(Co-authored with Walter Wriston)

Two of the supposed indicators of the economy's health—the trade deficit (or balance) and the federal budget deficit (or balance)—are constantly under the media spotlight, yet they are actually among the least important and most unreliable indicators that we have. This is not to say that each is unimportant, or that reaching a trade balance or a budget balance by 2002 would be unwelcome, but only that the two balances are among the least significant and most unreliable indicators of the economy's health and prospects.

Why then do they get so much attention in the media, in public discussion, and in political debate? If they are not so important, what are the other more important indicators of economic performance, and why do they receive so little attention?

The obvious answer to the first question is probably the most accurate one. Because the trade and budget balances appear to be simple, easy to measure and understand, they give politicians something to talk about that they and voters can readily relate to: "Your family has to keep a balanced budget—why not your government?" On examination, however, this turns out to be a case of looking for a lost key under the street light instead of where the key fell.

Another question is, why are these two balances really of less importance than their publicity would suggest? There is an unspoken, and

---

A slightly edited version was published in **The Wall Street Journal** *on June 19, 1997 under the same title.*

erroneous, assumption that a trade deficit is bad for a country's economy. Remember Pat Buchanan standing on the pier decrying Japanese imports? The facts are that economies often, and indeed typically, prosper while experiencing large trade deficits, and conversely, their performance can lag badly while they are amassing large trade surpluses.

A quick look at the record, as Al Smith used to say, illustrates the point: The economies of the United States, Hong Kong, and South Korea have all prospered for most of the past decade, and more recently Poland, the Philippines, Turkey, and Croatia have been doing likewise, while following the same pattern: high growth and substantial trade deficits. On the other side of the ledger, Japan and Russia exemplify the reverse trend—poor, lagging economic performance while running up large trade surpluses. The German and French economies reflect similar predicaments.

The explanation for these seemingly counterintuitive situations is that a trade deficit (i.e., an import surplus) often reflects the strong demands of a booming economy for investment, consumption, and intermediate goods. Conversely, a trade surplus often reflects the weak demands of a depressed, deflationary economy in which internal savings outstrip the availability of domestic opportunities for profitable investment.

Moreover, the way we measure a trade balance is an artifact of another age: Now, and in the future, much of what is labeled as trade represents transactions among the international subsidiaries of the same parent company. But even apart from measurement flaws, the trade balance implies very little that is important in divining the health of a nation's economy.

Similarly, the federal budget balance or deficit, despite the inflated political rhetoric of recent years, carries with it very little significance about the economy's performance and outlook. It does not take a rocket scientist, or a chess-playing machine, to know that tax revenues fall and transfer payments rise when the economy is doing poorly, and vice versa when the economy prospers. Putting aside the fact that if private companies measured their profit and loss the way the Federal Government keeps its books (i.e., by counting borrowing as revenue and running no capital account), they would no doubt attract attention from the criminal division of the SEC—the existence of a budget balance or deficit doesn't indicate anything crucial about the health of an economy.

One vital fact ignored by the budget balance—one which has great significance for the economy's overall performance—is the *level* of spending at which the balance (or deficit) occurs. For example, a budget deficit incurred at a spending level that represents a relatively (by modern standards) modest share of GDP, say 30 percent (the U.S. level), may be a much more favorable economic indicator than a budget balance that is incurred at a spending level that is a much larger share of the GDP, say 45–50 percent, as is the case in most European economies.

There is another important consideration overlooked in the debate about a balanced budget: the proportion of any given budget that is allocated for public investment in road and productive infrastructure, rather than in transfer payments.

So the federal budget balance, like the trade balance, is of limited significance in assessing the economic health of a nation. In the case of Japan, for example, it seems quite clear that the recently enacted tax increases, designed to reduce Japan's budget deficit, may hinder rather than help in getting that economy moving again, while tax reductions might contribute to such an outcome, even if the deficit rose as a consequence.

If the two balances, trade and federal, are not the most important and reliable indicators of economic performance and prospects, what are the preferable harbingers of things to come? These would include the rate of growth in productivity (both labor productivity and "total factor productivity") insofar as we are able to measure it in an economy in which information is a key input; the economy's "openness" to competition (in terms of numbers of new start-up firms, openness to competition from imports, and limited and clear regulatory restrictions); the level and growth of employment opportunities; the state and progress of the educational system; the stability and predictability of the money supply, the price level, and the currency's exchange value; the level and rates of change in domestic savings and investments; and, as a summary, aggregate measure, the economy's rate of real economic growth.

Each of these indicators, and the final one as an overall measure of economic performance, carries with it more significance with respect to how well an economy is doing and its future prospects than the twin balances that are typically in the media spotlight. These are not where the real keys to the economy are to be found. The real keys don't have a sound bite facility; they are harder to deal with, harder to measure, more difficult to explain and understand, and more complicated to discuss. "Why can't the Government balance its checkbook?" gets us where we live—especially since none of us could keep our own books on the government model and stay out of the poorhouse. But it is not the right question if we are really interested in how the economy is doing, and how it will do in the future.

Postaudit

The basic point remains valid: namely, that the trade and budget deficits are less significant indicators of an economy's health and progress than the dozen other indicators referred to at the end of the essay.

Chapter 15

TAXES, TRADE, AND GROWTH

After the Party conventions conclude in August, it can be expected, or at least hoped, that the presidential campaigns will turn to substantive issues like economic growth, employment, wages, taxes, and trade. If and when this occurs, the ensuing debate should address one of the most basic, as well as most important, relationships in economics: that between the savings-investment balance, on the one hand, and the trade balance (or, more accurately, the current account balance), on the other. To the extent that domestic savings fall short of domestic investment, the economy must import more than it exports. So, if the savings-investment balance is negative, then the economy's trade balance will also be negative.

The importance of this relationship transcends that of the balance between federal government expenditures and revenues—that is, the budget deficit. The budget deficit is one among several factors influencing the savings-investment balance. Other factors include the absolute amount of government spending (quite apart from the size of the budget deficit itself), tax and regulatory incentives to save and invest, monetary policy, and demographics.

The singular importance of the balance between domestic savings and domestic investment is due to several of its consequences, including the link it provides between the domestic and international economies. This balance maps directly into changes in American holdings of assets abroad, and to changes in assets held in the United

---

*A slightly edited version was published in **The Los Angeles Times** on August 11, 1996 under the title "How Do We Force Ourselves to Save More?"*

States by other governments, as well as by corporate and individual entities domiciled in other countries. Over time, the savings-investment balance determines whether the American economy earns more in interest and dividends from its foreign holdings than it pays to other economies on their holdings in the United States. This, in turn, determines whether the gross *national* product is larger or smaller than the gross *domestic* product. (The difference between GNP and GDP is net income received from, or paid to, the rest of the world: GNP is less than GDP when we pay more to the rest of the world than the income we receive from it, and vice versa).

Furthermore, the savings-investment balance significantly affects the growth of employment and wages, as well as the economy's overall rate of growth. Boosting domestic savings and investment—and, in particular, boosting savings by more than investment—is also of central importance for reversing the perennial U.S. pattern of importing capital from abroad to finance the excess of U.S. imports over its exports.

For the past decade, the United States has experienced a shortfall of gross domestic savings compared to gross domestic investment. This perennial shortfall has varied between 1 and 2 percent of the GDP, averaging about $100 billion annually from 1985 through 1995. This savings shortfall is reflected by the excess of U.S. imports of goods and services over our exports. As a consequence of the cumulative shortfall in annual savings, about 18 percent (about $750 billion) of total U.S. public debt is held abroad.

To improve the performance of the American economy, policies should be pursued that will increase both investment and savings, but will increase savings by more than the increase in investment—thereby reducing or reversing the savings shortfall referred to earlier. Accomplishing this goal would mean that the current account deficit of the past decade would be replaced by a current account surplus, that U.S. exports would increase by more than increases in imports, that additional and relatively high-paying jobs would be generated (because wages in exporting industries are about 15–18 percent above average wages), and that U.S. economic growth would rise. As a consequence, U.S. import of capital would be reversed and the burden of servicing foreign-held debt would be eased. Instead, U.S. exports of capital would result in our receiving net income from abroad, rather than incurring net servicing obligations to other countries.

So much for *what* needs to be done and *why*. The next question is *how* can this be done—that is, how can investment and savings be raised, while raising savings more than investment? Several options are worth considering—their respective economic merits may be uncorrelated, or even negatively correlated, with their political merits and political feasibility. One option would be a straight across-the-board reduction in marginal tax rates, perhaps by 5 percent, 5 percent, and 3 percent, corresponding to the three presently graduated marginal tax rates. The expanded tax base that such a change in marginal rates would create is likely to minimize the resulting reductions in revenue yields, and perhaps to avoid such reductions entirely.

A second option would focus more directly on incentives to save—for example, by eliminating taxation of interest and dividend income, and expanding the tax-deductibility of 401(k) contributions and IRAs (for example, to include non-working spouses as proposed in a bipartisan bill presently under consideration in Congress).

A third option is to move gradually toward an equitably-graduated consumption-based tax structure with exemptions and lower rates applying to smaller consumption outlays, and a higher rate applying to larger consumption outlays.

Some worry—not without reason—that a consumption-type system might generate a deluge of revenues, thereby tempting future Administrations and Congresses to increase spending. To ease this concern, a consumption-based system might be accompanied by automatic caps that would be triggered if revenues exceeded the standard 19–20 percent of GDP typically represented by federal government revenues over the past two decades.

Pursuing one or more of these options, while maintaining a suitably prudent set of monetary policies, will improve the economy's performance by raising annual growth—perhaps by 0.5 percent or 1.0 percent—from, say, 2.5 percent to 3.0 percent or 3.5 percent, thereby adding $35–70 billion annually to GDP. These cumulative additions, which would total $1 trillion by 2025, are of crucial importance if the

United States is to manage the prospective surge in social spending as the baby-boom generation matures.

Postaudit

The contention of this essay—that savings in the U.S. economy are low and should be encouraged—is no less valid but is distinctly less relevant in 2002, when the economy's growth appears to be demand-limited, than it was in the buoyant economy of 1996, when the essay was written.

Part III

Asian Economics and Politics

Chapter 16

ARE "ASIAN VALUES" REALLY THAT UNIQUE?

"Asian values" have been both extolled and censured by innumerable politicians, pundits, and professors in countless written and spoken words. The praise has been for the putative contribution of Asian values to the "miracle" of Asian economic development in the 1980s and through the mid-1990s. The blame has been for their putative contribution to Asia's financial meltdown in 1997 and 1998. Whether praising or blaming, these opposed commentaries have held two premises in common: first, that Asian values are pervasively shared among the dozen countries and 2.7 billion people in the Asian region (including India), and second, that these values are unique, hence distinctly different from "Western values."

This is the mythology about Asian values. The reality, strongly supported by recent empirical evidence, is that both premises are false. The values cherished by Asia's heterogeneous peoples, nations, and cultures are in fact very diverse, and much—indeed most—of what is valued highly in Asia is markedly similar to what is highly valued in the West!

Adherents of the mythology about Asian values typically cross familiar ideological and policy lines. On the one hand, those who laud Asian values, including Lee Kwan Yew in Singapore, Eisuke Sakakibara in Japan, and Mohamad Mahathir in Malaysia, typically stress the Confucian precepts of work, frugality, and hierarchy. These di-

*A slightly edited version was published in **The Los Angeles Times** on November 7, 1999 under the same title and in **The International Herald Tribune** on November 10, 1999 under the title "Asians' Values Seem Much Like Everyone Else's."*

mensions of Asian values, they contend, underlie the dramatic economic growth achieved in East Asia by Japan in the 1970s and 1980s, the four "Tigers" (Korea, Taiwan, Hong Kong, and Singapore) in the 1980s and mid-1990s, and the three aspiring Tigers (Thailand, Indonesia, and Malaysia) until the middle of 1997.

On the other hand, those who fault Asian values, such as Paul Krugman at MIT, point to other dimensions of Asian values as major contributors to Asia's financial meltdown from mid-1997 through 1998. According to this view, the sources of Asia's financial crisis can be traced to such values as excessive loyalty to family, clan, or otherwise favored "in-groups," leading to nepotism, cronyism, and corruption. From this perspective, Asian values are blamed for cumulative economic distortions and resource misallocations which in turn precipitated the Asian financial crisis in 1997.

Now that economic recovery is well underway in some parts of the previously afflicted region—notably, in South Korea and Thailand— it can be expected that the extollers of Asian values will be heard from once again.

In any event, whether Asian values are offered as explanations for positive economic performance or for malperformance, the arguments lack credibility. A recent survey by Japan's prestigious Dentsu Institute for Human Studies provides convincing evidence for separating the mythology about Asian values from the reality. The Dentsu survey was conducted among a stratified sample of households in 1998 in the capital cities of six Asian countries (Japan, China, South Korea, Thailand, and Singapore, plus Bombay in India), and in 1997 in five Western countries (the United Kingdom, France, Germany, Sweden, and the United States—New York rather than Washington was the survey's location in the United States).

Respondents were asked to evaluate the relative weight they place on nine specified attributes of what is "important in life." The nine were "financial wealth"; "acquiring high-quality goods"; "family relationships"; "success in work"; "mental relaxation"; "leisure activity"; "living for the present"; "striving to achieve personal goals"; and "having good relationships with others."

I have compared the Asian responses with the Western ones, to test whether there are significant differences between the average responses of the two groups, and whether there are significant differences between the groups in the spread or dispersion of their responses.

The average (mean) for the Asian responses is significantly different from that of the Western responses in only two of the nine dimensions of value. On the average, Asian respondents place somewhat greater importance on relationships with family than do Western respondents; and Western respondents accord somewhat greater importance to leisure activity than do Asian respondents.

Moreover, the dispersion (variance) in the Asian and Western groups' responses is quite similar, with only two exceptions. The Asian respondents vary more widely among themselves in the importance they assign to good relations with "others" (as distinct from families), and in the importance they assign to leisure activity, than do the Western respondents.

The conclusion that emerges from the Dentsu survey is clear and sharply different from the mythology. First, Asian values are decidedly more similar to Western values than is usually presumed to be the case; and second, for some dimensions of "values" Asians diverge more from one another than they do from respondents in the United States and Western Europe. Prevalent beliefs on both points represent conventional *lack* of wisdom!

How then does the rhetoric about Asian values relate to Asia's varied economic trajectories: high performance until 1997, sharp reversals in 1997 and 1998, and substantial though widely varying economic recovery in 1999 among those who were hardest hit by the 1997 crisis? The answer is that Asian values provide little if any explanation for this volatile record. Explanations lie instead in the more mundane realm of economic policies, practices, and institutions. The sources of Asia's progress, reversals, and recovery lie not in the realm of "values," but are to be found elsewhere: in the macroeconomic monetary and fiscal policies pursued by the various Asian countries; in their policies relating to the term structure of foreign debt; in their use of nonmarket-based rather than market-based modes of resource allocation; and in the impediments they've placed in the way of entrepreneurial activity—domestic as well as foreign.

The range of values in Asia allows ample room for good as well as bad policies, for those promoting economic growth, as well as those impeding it. One does not have to look for deeper cultural or other explanations to understand how and why the respective Asian countries have come so far, nor why they have faltered and made serious missteps along the way.

Postaudit

Much of the earlier rhetoric about Asian values has become more subdued in light of economic reversals experienced by Japan and the former Asian "tigers." The essay's data and analysis seem to me equally as valid now as when the piece was written.

Chapter 17

THROUGH A HAZY CRYSTAL BALL: ASIA'S ECONOMIC OUTLOOK, 1997–2020

1. The Hazards of Forecasting

According to Niels Bohr, "It is very difficult to make predictions, especially about the future"! The wisdom of this precept is reinforced when forecasts are made for a region as diverse, dynamic, and volatile as Asia. This diversity is reflected in the enormous differences that prevail in the region's economic levels and rates of growth in GDP and per capita GDP, in technological sophistication, trading patterns and trading partners, capital flows, and even "cultural values."[1]

Because of this diversity, different growth trajectories can be expected both among the Asian countries and by each of them over time. So, China, Japan, India, Indonesia, and Korea may experience very different growth patterns over the next two decades.

A striking example of both variability and volatility in the region is provided by the sharply different impact that Asia's financial turmoil

---

A slightly edited version was published in **Jobs and Capital**, *Winter 1998, under the same title.*

[1]Despite the frequent proclamations by Mahathir Mohamad and Lee Kuan Yew about "Asian values," the proposition that these values are either homogeneous within the region, or strikingly different from cultural values prevailing elsewhere, is really a myth. Consider, for example, how sharp are the cultural differences between, say, Indonesia and Japan, or how similar is the entrepreneurial zeal that one finds in, say, South China and Korea on the one hand, and Silicon Valley on the other!

has had since mid-1997 on one indicator of the economic outlook—
namely, the national stock markets in the region. On a year-over-year
basis in December 1997, Japan's Nikkei index had fallen 12 percent,
Hong Kong's Hang Seng index 20 percent, Korea's 57 percent, Thailand's 72 percent, Malaysia's 71 percent, and Indonesia's 60 percent,
while Taiwan's index increased 7 percent and China's increased by
35 percent.[2]

2. A Base-Line Forecast

Over the past decade, RAND has done several studies of the outlook
for the Asian economies, as well as their security environment, compared with those of the United States and western Europe. The first
of these studies was done in 1987 for the National Commission on
Integrated Long-Term Strategy and published in April 1989,[3] the second was done in 1994, and published in 1995.[4]

In characterizing the Asian economic outlook, the studies focused on
two salient indicators—gross domestic product, and per capita GDP.
(The Asian security outlook was characterized in terms of two other
salient indicators—military spending and military investment.) For
this essay, the economic indicators are germane, despite their limitations. For example, they do not directly reflect such other important dimensions of economic performance as sectoral growth patterns, transnational corporate business alliances and technology
transactions, trade patterns, and capital flows. Nevertheless, the GDP
and per capita GDP forecasts provide a useful starting point for assessing the region's economic outlook.

The RAND studies used a closed macroeconomic model for each
country to estimate its future GDP growth, based on rates of growth

---

[2]Because the yuan is not fully convertible, the Chinese index is not strictly comparable
to the others.

[3]See Charles Wolf Jr., Gregory Hildebrandt, Michael Kennedy, et al. *Long-Term Economic and Military Trends, 1950–2010.*" RAND N-2757-USDP, 1989.

[4]Charles Wolf Jr. and K.C. Yeh. *Long-Term Economic and Military Trends, 1994–2015:
The United States and Asia.* RAND MR-627-OSD, 1995. Several smaller studies, based
on and updating these earlier ones have also been done: see for example, Charles Wolf
Jr., *China as an Emerging Economic Super Power?* presented at a symposium held in
Shanghai in June 1997; and "Asia 2015." *Wall Street Journal,* March 20, 1997.

in the capital stock, in employed labor, and in total factor productivity. The outlook for productivity growth in the respective economies was estimated from their experienced growth during the previous decade combined with explicit judgments by the RAND team as to whether the future would replicate or diverge from the prior time trend. The United States and Germany were also included in the studies for comparative purposes, with Germany representing a surrogate for the entire European Union, as described below.

The principal results of these studies are summarized in Table 17.1 and Figures 17.1 and 17.2.

As Table 17.1 indicates, the estimates made in 1987 and 1995 correspond closely, with Korea as the major exception. The 1995 Korean forecast was biased upwards by certain premature, if not unrealistic, assumptions about the timing and process of reunification in the peninsula. In general, with the exception of Korea and probably also the United States, the 1995 estimates provide a more accurate indication of what the aggregate economic outlook in the region will be.

Table 17.1

**Forecasted Annual GDP Growth Rates,
1997-2015: Principal Asian Economies,
United States, and Germany (%)**

	Estimates Made in 1987	Estimates Made in 1995
China	4.7	4.0[a]
Japan	2.9	2.5
Korea	4.9	7.1
India	4.0	5.5
Indonesia	[b]	5.0
Taiwan	5.7	5.3
Germany	2.1	2.3
United States	2.6	2.2

SOURCES: See references in footnotes 3 and 4 to cited RAND studies.

[a]The estimate for China is the mean of two alternative scenarios—one involving sustained growth, the other interrupted growth.

[b]Indonesia was not included in the 1987 RAND study.

Perhaps the most striking divergence between the Asian economic outlook depicted in Figure 1 and the more or less "consensus" view portrayed by other sources is the slower, though still substantial, growth we have estimated for China. The 4 percent figure shown in the 1995 estimate for China represents about half that of recent estimates by the World Bank and other sources. As previously noted, the 1995 figure shown for China in Table 1 is the average of an "optimistic" scenario leading to a growth rate of about 5 percent annually, and a "pessimistic" scenario for which the estimate was 3 percent.

Several major factors account for the slowdown forecasted for China:

- Implementation by China of an explicit government policy designed to transfer income from high growth and relatively wealthy Eastern provinces to the poorer Western ones, probably resulting in raising consumption at the expense of savings for the Chinese economy as a whole;

- Probably modest reductions in the inflow of capital and associated technology and management from "maritime" Chinese and other sources, including Taiwan, Hong Kong, and Southeast Asia;[5]

- A rising capital-output ratio for new investment in China due to several influences: for example, investments in transportation and other capital-intensive infrastructure projects; the enormous and costly Three Gorges multi-purpose dams; large continuing construction costs in Shanghai and other urban areas; probable increased energy costs; and the need to reduce or reverse environmental effects of water and atmospheric pollution;

- Potential increases in military spending.

---

[5]During the first half of the 1990s, China has been the principal recipient of long-term capital inflows from the rest of the world, at an annual rate of about $40 billion, representing 20–25 percent of the global total. In the coming decades, while China is likely to continue to be an attractive venue for private long-term foreign investment, the proportion of this capital inflow and its magnitude in real dollars is likely to decrease somewhat. See the author's "Global Competition for Long-Term Capital: Who Will Win?" *Business Economics*, July 1996.

On the other hand, it is possible that successful privatization of China's burdensome State-Owned Enterprises could have a countervailing effect on China's future growth, offsetting some of the growth-inhibiting factors mentioned above.

Figure 17.1 shows the aggregate GDP figures for the Asian countries corresponding to the 1995 growth rates shown in Table 17.1.

The estimates shown in Figure 17.1 are expressed in terms of the relative buying power (i.e., purchasing power) of the respective national currencies converted to 1997 U.S. dollars. Use of these PPP exchange rates has a major effect on the *levels* (but not the growth rates) of the corresponding estimates for each country, compared to what these estimates would be if the GDP figures were instead based

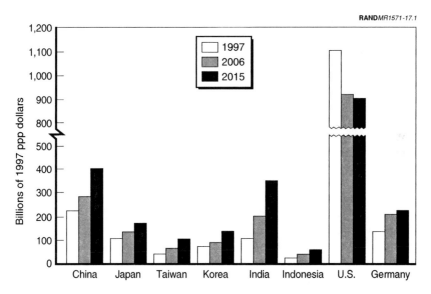

SOURCE: Updated from Charles Wolf and K. C. Yeh. *Long-Term Economic and Military Trends*, 1994–2015, RAND, 1995, using U.S. GDP deflator (annual average, 1993–1996, = 2.27%) to express estimates in 1997 dollars.

Figure 17.1—GDP Estimates for Asian Countries, Germany, and the United States, 1997–2015

on nominal foreign exchange (FX) rates. For example, if FX rates were used for the conversion into dollars instead of the PPP rates, the GDP estimates for China would be only one-sixth of those shown in Figure 17.1, while the estimates for Japan would be about 80 percent *higher* than those shown in Figure 17.1.

It can be expected that over the next two decades these large discrepancies between the PPP and FX exchange rates will narrow, if and as the respective countries become more open to trade and capital flows. Consequently, the PPP-based estimates for China will probably turn out to be somewhat less than those shown in Figure 17.1, while the corresponding FX-based estimates will be somewhat more than the one-sixth ratio mentioned above. Conversely, the GDP estimates for Japan will very likely turn out to be higher than the level shown in Figure 1, while the corresponding FX-based estimates for Japan will be somewhat lower than those cited earlier.

With these caveats in mind, several points can be inferred from Figure 17.1 concerning the outlook for the Asian economies in relation to the global economy and to the economies of other countries.

- China's GDP, like that of the United States, will be about one-fourth of the global gross product in 2015.[6]

- By 2015, China's GDP dollar equivalent will be more than twice that of Japan, while Japan's GDP will be about twice that of Korea.

- The five principal Asian economies (China, Japan, India, Korea, and Indonesia) will constitute about 45 percent of the global economy, on the assumption that Germany's GDP remains about 40 percent of that of the entire European Union whose combined GDP will shrink to about 15 percent of the global product.

---

[6]It is also worth noting that the GDP growth rate shown for China in Table 16.1, representing the average of the estimated growth rates for the two China scenarios referred to earlier, is less than half the corresponding estimates made by the World Bank, and considerably less than half China's reported real growth rates during the past decade.

- The GDP of the United States will be about 25 percent of the global product (about the same proportion as at present), and about the same proportion as that of China in 2015.

- Finally, the economy of India in 2015 will be about 60 percent as large as that of the entire European Union, according to the estimates shown in Figure 17.1.

Another way of scaling the Asian economic outlook is to show how its per capita GDP estimates compare with those of other countries. These estimates are shown in Figure 17.2.

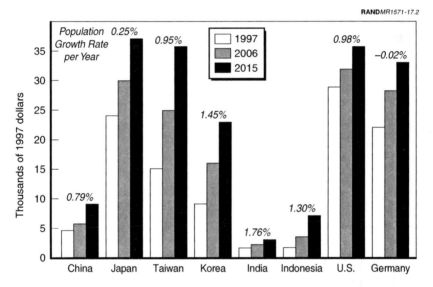

SOURCE: Charles Wolf and K. C. Yeh. *Long-Term Economic and Military Trends*, 1994–2015, RAND, 1995; Charles Wolf and Michael Kennedy. "Long-Term Economic & Military Trends, 1994–2015: Russia, Germany, and Indonesia," unpublished paper.

Figure 17.2—Per Capita GDP Estimates for Asian Countries, Germany, and the United States

Figure 17.2 presents a very different picture from that portrayed in Figure 17.1—a picture that can be summarized as follows:

- The per capita estimates for the United States, Japan, Germany, and Taiwan are about equal as of 2015—between $33,000 and $37,000.

- The per capita figures for each of these "rich" countries are about four times that of China, while the per capita figure for Korea (about $23,000 for the reunified country) reaches about two-thirds that of the "rich" countries.

- Of the countries shown in Figure 17.2, the lowest per capita figures are those of China, Indonesia, and India—China's per capita GDP will be about $9,000, while that of India will be about one-third, and Indonesia about three-quarters, that of China.

3. Alternative Views of the Asian Economic Outlook

Views about Asia's economic future are divided, if not polarized, between pessimists and optimists. In the United States the pessimists are well represented by Paul Krugman of MIT, while the optimists are no less effectively represented by Jeffrey Sachs of Harvard. Krugman's pessimism antedates the bursting of Asia's "bubble" since mid-1997, so he can claim some degree of prescience. Moreover, the number of adherents to this view, including numerous international money managers, has enormously increased since then. Sachs's optimism, which is endorsed by the World Bank as well as the Asian Development Bank, preceded the recent turmoil in Asian financial markets, but has been sustained since then.

Both of these positions leave something to be desired—Krugman's perhaps a bit more than Sachs's. As the data summarized in Table 17.1 and Figures 17.1 and 17.2 above suggest, my views are less buoyant than those of Sachs and the World Bank, yet not so far from these views as are Krugman's. My views can perhaps be aptly characterized as "realistically optimistic," somewhat closer to Sachs's views than to Krugman's.

Krugman's pessimistic view, based on empirical work done by Alwyn Young, Laurence Lau, and Jong-Il Kim, can be summarized in the following propositions:

1. Most of Asia's seemingly "miraculous" growth over the past two decades has been due to the growth of capital and labor inputs, rather than to increases in productivity of these inputs.

2. This pattern contrasts with the development experience of the West, in which increased productivity, rather than simply mobilizing large quantities of inputs, accounted for much of the realized growth.

3. So, it can be inferred that Asia's future growth will sharply decline, because the accumulation of inputs will slow down and because these will be subject to diminishing returns.

There are several flaws in this argument.

First, in the RAND work referred to earlier, we found a distinctly mixed picture among the various Asian countries with respect to the relative contribution of productivity growth and input growth in accounting for GDP growth during the past decade. For example, annual growth in total factor productivity in Japan ranged between a slightly negative and a slightly positive figure over the period; in China the corresponding productivity growth was about 1.5 percent per annum; in Korea it ranged between 2 percent and 3 percent; in India about 1.5 percent; and in Indonesia the corresponding figure was approximately 1.3 percent. The underlying data for all these estimates are admittedly soft. But the picture that emerges is more mixed than Krugman suggests: in some of the Asian countries, productivity growth has been appreciable, in others it has been minimal.

Second, to the extent that productivity growth in some Asian countries has indeed been minimal, quite a different inference can be drawn from that which Krugman suggests. If in fact these efficiency gains have been less in Asia than has been characteristic of development in the West, this can just as plausibly be construed as providing greater opportunities for future productivity growth, rather than foreclosing them.

Finally, it can be convincingly argued that the prospect for a continuation of high savings and investment rates, and for large increases in employed labor, remain strong in Asia. The extraordinary mobilization of inputs that the Asian countries have manifested in the past is not unlikely to be sustained in the future.

On the other hand, Sachs and his World Bank and Asian Development Bank associates may be somewhat more optimistic than is warranted. The World Bank has projected annual economic growth in the Asia-Pacific region at about 7.7 percent (hence, per capita GDP growth would be about 5 percent or 5.5 percent), and China's growth at slightly above 8 percent (hence, its per capita annual GDP growth would be 6.5 percent to 7 percent). Sachs's own estimates are slightly lower than those of the Bank: for example, in a recent article on "Asia's Reemergence," he forecasts China's annual rate of growth in per capita GDP between 1996 and 2025 at 6.0 percent.[7] These estimates are considerably higher than those advanced in Table 17.1 and Figure 17.2 above.

So, Sachs's estimates of Asia's economic outlook seem to me overly optimistic for several reasons. As Asia's growth proceeds, long-deferred per capita consumption may rise. While Asia's savings rates will surely remain high by Western standards, they very likely will decrease from the extraordinarily high levels experienced in the past decade. Moreover, Asia's access to foreign capital, and the invaluable management and technology associated with it, may become more constrained in the coming decades. This may ensue as a consequence of the huge losses in Asian market values experienced by foreign equity investors since the middle of 1997, as well as the emergence of alternative opportunities for profitable foreign investment and trade in Latin America, Eastern Europe, and Russia.

4. Consequences and Implications of Asia's 1997 Financial Turmoil

As noted earlier, the value of stock market capitalizations in most of the Asian countries experienced enormous losses in 1997. Expressed in U.S. dollars the losses are magnified due to significant currency depreciations in all cases except Hong Kong where the dollar peg has held, and mainland China where the yuan is not fully convertible. Perhaps the sharp divergences among the China, Hong Kong, and Taiwan indexes suggest that the standard mantra of "one China and two systems" should be recast instead as "one China, *three* systems"!

---

[7]Stephen Radelet and Jeffrey Sachs. "Asia's Reemergence." *Foreign Affairs,* November/December 1997.

While these developments represent a serious setback from the previous optimism about Asia's economic outlook, it remains to be seen how long the setback will endure. Its duration and consequent effect on future foreign direct investment, portfolio equity investment, and long-term lending will depend on certain key institutional developments, as well as on the macroeconomic indicators—monetary policy and fiscal policy—that economists typically emphasize.

Among these key institutional developments, two related ones are of central importance:

- a clear, reliable legal structure, including the delineation of property rights, and greater transparency and predictability of regulatory and tax measures;

- sound financial institutions, including a banking industry whose lending reflects rigorous, explicit, and even-handed banking criteria (rather than "crony," preferential ones), and equity markets that are open and competitive.

For sustained and high growth, and a generally favorable economic outlook in Asia, the discipline of competitive markets should govern allocation of resources, rather than the leniency and favoritism of political, family, or "crony" connections. This imperative is not an issue of equity versus efficiency, or morality versus economics. In this case, tradeoffs between these pairs are not involved because the pairs move in the same direction. Efficiency and equity trade"on" rather than "off."

In the wake of Asia's financial turmoil in 1997, we have seen the emergence of several multilateral "bailout" funds. Under the aegis and leadership of the International Monetary Fund, these safety-nets for Thailand and Indonesia amount to more than $40 billion. A similar fund of this magnitude may also be created for Korea. The magnitude and proliferation of this instrumentality carries with it both positive and negative implications.

On the positive side, the creation of such substantial financial cushions can significantly contribute to boosting investors' confidence and expectations, reducing or reversing incentives for asset-holders to divest their holdings, relieving pressure on currency and equities markets, and avoiding or at least damping the risk of serious deflationary effects in non-Asian markets, as well.

On the other hand, the creation of these bailouts can have negative and perverse consequences. For example, the conditions that the IMF typically attaches to the creation and use of these funds usually emphasize reductions in internal budget and current account deficits, as proxies for appropriate macroeconomic, fiscal, and monetary policies. IMF conditionality usually gives less attention to other measures, such as reducing government spending, decreasing the size of the public sector, and reducing government employment. Moreover, the building of sounder legal and financial institutions, which I have stressed, usually receives secondary attention by the Fund.

Furthermore, bailout funds may create moral hazards of two types. One type involves a possible incentive for governments to eschew sound macroeconomic policies and institution-building efforts because of a belief that the bailout option will be available if things go awry. The second type may lead governments to defer taking remedial measures as quickly as they otherwise would do.

The existence of moral hazards probably warrants more sparing use of these bailout measures than seems to be currently favored. Their excessive use would not be the first time that good intentions have had perverse consequences.

Postaudit

The forecasts seem to me to deserve no better than a B+! Growth rates for Korea and Indonesia seem too high, that for the United States probably is too low. The moral hazard problem remains a serious concern.

Chapter 18

ASIA IN 2015

What will Asia look like in the second decade of the twenty-first century? While no one knows, this doesn't mean all guesses are equally good. To get a better fix on the future, a promising place to start is with three key indicators of the future economic and military position of the principal Asian countries including—besides the United States—China, Japan, Korea, Indonesia, and India. Inclusion of India is based on the premise that its size, growth, and history will make it increasingly influential in the broad Asian region in the twenty-first century.

The three key indicators are gross domestic product (GDP), per capita GDP, and military capital—military capital is the accumulated cost of new military procurement, *plus* spending on military research and development, and *minus* depreciation of the previously accumulated stock of military capital. To be sure, there are many other important indicators of what the future of Asia will look like. For example, trade and investment flows will both portend and affect the future, as will the leadership successions in China and Indonesia, China's management of Hong Kong, the relationship between Taiwan and the mainland, and the process of reunification in Korea.

Nevertheless, these three key quantitative indicators provide a good place to begin consideration of what the future Asian environment will look like. All of the estimates summarized below are based on a recently published RAND study, using exchange rates that reflect the

---

*A slightly edited version was published in **The Wall Street Journal** on March 20, 1997 under the same title.*

"real" purchasing power of the respective currencies expressed in 1997 U.S. dollars, rather than the nominal current exchange rates of these currencies.

In 2015, China's GDP will reach between 11 and 12 trillion U.S. dollars. This estimate is the average of two alternative scenarios for China's growth in the intervening period: one positing stable and sustained growth, and the other envisaging slower, interrupted growth. Even in the higher growth scenario, we envisaged an appreciable slowing in China's growth rates from the extremely high levels of the 1980s and 1990s. This slowing, which would still leave China with a substantial average annual growth rate between 4 and 5 percent (compared to World Bank estimates of 8 percent), is due to several factors: higher initial GDP (so a specified percentage growth requires larger annual increments), government policy explicitly designed to transfer wealth from the high-growth eastern provinces to poorer western ones, and a modest reduction in the inflow of capital to the mainland from overseas Chinese sources. (Hong Kong and Taiwan are not included in the estimates for China.)

The corresponding forecast for the GDP of the United States is about the same as that for China—between 11 and 12 trillion dollars—compared with the current annual U.S. GDP of about 7.5 trillion. The forecasts for the other major Asian countries are shown in Table 18.1. The estimates shown in the table compare with current GDP levels of about $5 trillion for China, $3 trillion for Japan, $1.3 trillion for India, $430 billion for Korea, and $545 billion for Indonesia.

Table 18.1

Gross Domestic Products, 2015
(in trillions of 1997 U.S. dollars)

United States	11–12
China	11–12
Japan	4–5
India	4
Korea	2
Indonesia	1.5–2.0

SOURCE: Charles Wolf and K. C. Yeh. *Long-Term Economic and Military Trends, 1994–2015,* 1995.

Two other benchmarks are useful for sizing these forecasts. Using the same forecasting model, the RAND study estimated that Germany's GDP will reach about $2.7 trillion in 2015, compared to about $1.7 trillion at present. Assuming that Germany's GDP is about 40 percent of that of the European Union, the Asian countries shown in the table, including the United States, will comprise about 70 percent of the global product, while that of the European Union will be about 15 percent.

By 2015, the GDP of the United States will represent about a quarter of the global economy, about the same proportion as at the present time. China's economy, which will also constitute about a quarter of the global product in 2015, will be about twice as large as that of Japan, and Korea's GDP will be half that of Japan. India's GDP will, by 2015, be about 60 percent as large as that of the European Union.

Based on population estimates from United Nations and national sources, per capita GDP estimates for 2015 show, not surprisingly, a very different picture. Japan's per capita GDP will reach about $36,000, about the same as that of the United States (and Germany), while China's per capita GDP will be about one quarter of this figure. Korea's reunified 80 million population will reach about two-thirds of the per capita figure of the richer countries, while per capita GDP in India will be only 40 percent that of China, and Indonesia's per capita GDP (about $6,600) will be nearly twice that of India.

Use of military capital as a relevant indicator requires explanation. Military capital is only a partial and imperfect indicator of effective military capabilities. These depend on much more than procurement of military hardware, and spending on military research and development. Military capabilities also depend on training, leadership, morale, and command and control of military forces. And, of course, military capabilities themselves do not indicate much about either the intentions or purposes for which these capabilities may be used.

Nevertheless, despite its limitations, the accumulation of military capital does provide one salient indicator of military power. Estimated military capital in 2015, drawn from the same RAND study as Table 18.1, is summarized in Table 18.2.

Table 18.2

Military Capital, 2015
(in billions of 1997 dollars)

United States	895
China	410
Japan	173
Korea	129
India	353
Indonesia	60

Except for the United States estimate, all of the military capital stock figures represent substantial increases from the corresponding 1997 levels. For example, the estimates for China and Japan are about double their present levels, while the estimate for India is nearly four times its present figure. For the United States, the 2015 military capital estimate is actually about 25 percent *less* than the current level, because annual depreciation of the large existing military capital stocks of the United States is likely to exceed new military procurement in the intervening years.

These estimates of GDP, per capita GDP, and military capital provide a partial answer to the question of what Asia will look like in 2015:

1. The economies and military scale of the principal Asian countries will grow substantially, relative to those of the rest of the world.

2. The GDP and military capital of China will become relatively large, while its per capita GDP will remain relatively low.

3. India will reach a substantially increased economic and military scale in the Asian   region.

4. The economic and military capabilities of a reunified Korea will increase relative to those of Japan.

5. The economic and military position of the United States in Asia will remain prominent, although its relative scale will be reduced.

6. China's position in the region, though greatly enhanced, will be modulated by several factors: notably, an appreciable slowing of its high rate of growth during the last decade, and the counterweights presented by Japan, India, Korea, and Indonesia, as well as the United States.

Postaudit

The only estimates and conclusions in this essay that warrant a significant change are those relating to the United States. Developments since 9/11 would call for increasing rather than reducing the relative U.S. standing.

Chapter 19

THE ACCUMULATION OF MILITARY CAPITAL IN ASIA
AND THE UNITED STATES, 1997–2015

The relation between economic growth and military resource allocations is complex. On the one hand, more rapid growth and a larger
gross domestic product (GDP) increases resources available for military spending. On the other hand, larger allocations for military purposes may slow economic growth, to the extent that such allocations
reduce non-military capital formation. Moreover, the scale of military resource allocations usually depends on the existence of security
threats or uncertainties, and this influence on military spending may
be unrelated to economic growth.

Over the past decade, and prior to the financial turmoil in Asia since
the middle of 1997, RAND has engaged in several studies of long-
term economic and military trends, focusing on four salient indicators of these trends: namely, GDP; per capita GDP; military spending;
and military capital (the latter defined as procurement of new
weapons systems, either from domestic production or through imports of military equipment, *minus* the depreciation of the previously
accumulated military capital stock). The forecasting model used in
this work explicitly linked growth of GDP to military spending, and
military spending to military capital through the proportion of military spending devoted to procurement of military equipment, as distinct from current operations and maintenance costs.

*A slightly edited version was published in the **National Strategy Reporter**, Winter 1998,
under the title "The Power Equation: Military Capital in East Asia and the United
States, 1997–2015."*

The results of these calculations are summarized in Figure 19.1.

Several important cautionary observations should be made about these estimates. As noted on the vertical axis, the dollar estimates of military capital are expressed in purchasing power parity (ppp) dollars rather than nominal FX rates. It may be less appropriate to use ppp exchange rates rather than nominal FX rates in making comparisons of military capital across countries, than, for example, in making inter-country comparisons of GDP, or per capita GDP. To the extent that acquisitions of military capital are procured at world market prices, clearly the FX rates would represent the appropriate conversion metric, rather than the ppp rate. On the other hand, a counter argument can also be made: for example, to the extent that China acquires new military equipment from its own defense indus-

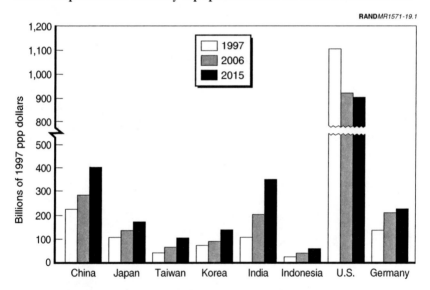

RAND*MR1571-19.1*

SOURCE: Updated from Charles Wolf and K. C. Yeh. *Long-Term Economic and Military Trends*, 1994–2015, RAND, 1995, using U.S. GDP deflator (annual average, 1993–1996, = 2.27%) to express estimates in 1997 dollars.

Figure 19.1—Military Capital Estimates, 1997–2015

tries at RMB-based prices, or through quasi-barter transactions with Russia, the ppp rate would still retain validity.

Moreover, military capital itself—even if the estimates shown in the bar chart are accurate—is a highly imperfect and incomplete indicator of military capabilities, let alone of intentions relating to their use. Even if our estimates were accurate, military capital is only one of the many inputs affecting military capabilities, and the effect of capital on military capabilities depends heavily on these other inputs. They include, for example, training and morale; command, communications, control, and intelligence; military leadership and doctrine; and maintenance and logistics support. These other ingredients are not readily inferred from the estimates of military capital accumulations, and they are also ones in which the effectiveness and competitive position of China and most of the other Asian countries are relatively weak. The pace at which these other ingredients will be upgraded in the coming years, and hence will be able to complement military capital accumulations in the development of effective military power, is a key issue which is not addressed in our calculations.

Notwithstanding the limitations that I've noted, some interesting inferences can be drawn from the data shown in the chart:

- Between 1997 and 2015, the military capital stocks of China and Japan will approximately double, while India's military capital will nearly quadruple over the same period.

- While the U.S. military capital stock still predominates in the global balance, its relevant weight decreases for two reasons: first, the U.S. military capital estimate for 2015 is actually about 25 percent less than the current level, because annual depreciation of its large existing military capital stocks exceeds new military procurement in the intervening years; and second, the build-up of military capital by the other countries shown in the chart increases their absolute and hence their relative stocks of military capital. (Of course, the estimates that we've made are based on an estimating methodology that begs the crucial question of technology and quality embodied in the dollar figures. Whether the so-called "revolution in military affairs" will enable the United States to maintain or even enhance its qualitative advantage over other countries, notwithstanding a smaller relative

dollar value, is an important matter that is not adequately reflected in the estimating methodology we used.)

As previously noted, the estimates shown in the chart preceded the
massive financial turmoil that has occurred throughout the Asia-
Pacific region since the middle of 1997. These financial shocks will
strongly, as well as differentially, affect military spending, procurement, research and development, defense production and imports in
Japan, China, Korea, Taiwan, Indonesia, Southeast Asia, and India. In
turn, these differences will affect military procurement and modernization, military capabilities, and the balance of military forces
within the region. There also may be significant effects on the willingness and ability of Japan and Korea to continue to pay the large
share of current stationing costs of U.S. forces based in Japan. Currently, over 75 percent of these costs are borne by Japan, and 64 percent of the costs of U. S. forces based in Korea are borne by Korea,
compared to much smaller proportions of the stationing costs paid
by U.S. allies in NATO. Whether a change in this burden-sharing with
Japan and Korea may occur and, if it does, whether it might in turn
affect the size of U.S. forward-based forces in these countries are key
issues that could have a major impact on the balance of military
forces in the region, on stability in the Korean peninsula, and on the
circumstances surrounding other possible contingencies in the region.

In reflecting on the relation between the financial turmoil in Asia and
the military outlook in the region, one striking fact is worth noting.
Among the set of Asian economies, the two countries that have
weathered the shocks with relative success are China and Taiwan.
China's restricted Shanghai and Shenzhen stock markets have actually risen in market value calculated in China's own currency, and
Taiwan's market capitalizations have actually risen. The Chinese currency, which is convertible only on current account and not on capital account, has been stable, and Taiwan's dollar has depreciated
only about 15 percent (compared with 30 percent depreciation of the
Japanese yen, and 70–80 percent depreciation of the Southeast Asian
currencies). China's relative stability in the face of the Asian shocks
has been preserved by allowing only limited convertibility of the
RMB, restricting foreign access to its securities markets, maintaining
a large current account surplus, and enormously increasing its reserves (from about $88 billion to about $140 billion on a year-over-

year basis). Taiwan, on the other hand, has managed to reconcile a relatively open economy with economic stability in the face of the regional financial shocks by a set of very different measures: a prudent and restrained monetary policy (M-2 increased only 10 percent on a year-over-year basis versus 127 percent in China), near-zero inflation, flexible foreign exchange rates, and a high ratio of foreign direct investment to foreign portfolio investment.

Although China and Taiwan have thus followed very different policies and used very different instruments in maintaining their stability in the face of enormous volatility among their neighbors, the result is that both of them are in a better position to sustain, modernize, and enhance their military capabilities and their military capital stocks than are their neighbors. Whether this fact will exert a stabilizing or destabilizing influence is a key issue for assessing the region's future security environment.

Postaudit

Reliable estimates of military capital are harder to make, but no less important than, estimates of downstream military spending as indicators of the military capabilities of different countries. These military capital forecasts still seem reasonable, although post 9/11 they underestimate the relative U.S. standing.

Chapter 20

TOO MUCH GOVERNMENT CONTROL

Asia's financial earthquake is the second biggest international surprise of the past decade. The first (and weightier one) was the demise of the Soviet Union. Like the 1991 Soviet shock, Asia's financial hemorrhaging has had many contributory causes. Most of these have been acknowledged and discussed, with the debate largely focusing on their relative importance.

However, the primary cause of the Asian crisis has been largely obscured: namely, the legacy of the so-called "Japan development model," and its perverse consequences. Subsequently relabelled the "Asian development model," because variants of it were applied elsewhere in the region, this strategy of economic growth has been grandly extolled in the past two decades. Its strongest proponents included Eisuke Sakakibara, presently Japan's vice minister of finance, Malaysia's prime minister Mahathir Mohamad, such Western commentators as Karel van Wolferen, Chalmers Johnson, James Fallows, Clyde Prestowitz, and numerous Western academics. What is now being witnessed in Asia's financial turbulence are the model's accumulated shortcomings.

This is not to deny the role of other proximate causes, but rather to suggest that many of them are traceable to or abetted by the primary one. The proximate causes, on which most discussion has focussed, include:

---

*A slightly edited version was published in **The Wall Street Journal** on February 4, 1998 under the same title.*

- Short-term foreign borrowing by Asian banks and companies, and long-term lending or investing; and in some instances re-lending to other countries or companies in the region. (The same point can, with equal validity, be reformulated to place the onus not on the Asian borrowers, but on the money center banks in Japan, the United States, and Germany that provided the mounting short-term lending to duly-anointed Asian countries and companies.)

- The assumption (by foreign investors) that exchange rates pegged to the U.S. dollar would be maintained—an unrealistic assumption because the dollar pegs depended on forms of capital inflow to the region (namely, short-term lending and portfolio investment) that are readily reversible, rather than direct investment, which is not.

Once these are acknowledged as proximate causes, how does the formerly-celebrated Japan model figure as the principal underlying explanation for Asia's financial predicament?

The model began with a conceptual framework largely provided by American and Japanese academic economists. Central to it is the phenomenon of "market failure": the predictable inability of market mechanisms to achieve maximum efficiency and to encourage growth when confronting "economies of scale" and "path dependence." These conditions may lead to monopolies in the advanced economies and the extinction of competition from late-starters in the development process. If the objectively-based decisions of the marketplace are recognized to have such predictable shortcomings, so the argument has run, then subjectively-based decisions by government agencies or key individuals could be expected to improve upon market outcomes.

In the original version of the model, these subjective judgments were provided by Japan's Ministry of International Trade and Industry (MITI) and its Ministry of Finance, in collaboration with particular targeted export industries believed to be associated with economies of scale. These priority "winners" were tagged to receive preferred access to capital, as well as protection in domestic markets through the use of non-tariff or tariff barriers to limit foreign competition.

In the Korean variant of the model, the subjective judgments as to who and what would receive preferment (often the same industries targeted by Japan), were exercised by a combination of the presidential Blue House, the benefitting *chaebol* conglomerates, and their associated and accommodating banks.

And in the Indonesian variant, the subjective oracular sources have been the presidency and its associated family lineage, in conjunction with the *soi disant* technological community in the Ministry of Research and Technology, led by its minister H. J. Habibie.

The common characteristic in all three versions is substitution of the objective, if sometimes imperfect, decisions of the market by the subjective judgments of government bureaucracies and influential individuals. These judgments then provided the basis for making allocative decisions as to which industries, firms, and individuals should get access to resources, and under what terms.

To be sure, the Japanese model and its variants produced noteworthy accomplishments. Vast amounts of savings and investment were mobilized for and channeled to the anointed industries and firms. While substantial resources were wasted in the process—for example, MITI's blunders in the case of steel, shipbuilding, and aircraft—the scale of resource commitments led to world-class performance in other cases—notably, cars, consumer electronics, telecommunications, and semiconductors in Japan, similar heavy industry development in Korea, and light industry development in Indonesia.

But the negative effects of the Asian model were cumulatively enormous, even though often obscured by the apparent successes. The principal negative effects include the following:

* Wasting of resources when mistaken decisions were made by the non-market choice processes. Indonesia's abortive investments in a national car and in a domestic aircraft industry are examples. These "*non*-market" failures account for the fact, stressed by several academic economists, that Asia's economic growth has been mainly due to large inputs of capital and labor, with relatively limited improvement in factor productivity.

* Structural imbalances within the Asian countries due to overemphasis on export industries and neglect of the domestic econ-

omy. As a result, domestic production has been short-changed, and consumption standards held down in favor of aggressive pursuit of export markets.

- Excess capacity has been built up in export industries through the arbitrary processes of picking "winners." Failure to take adequate account of demand saturation while production continued to expand has contributed to currency depreciation, falling prices, and sharply adverse changes in Asia's terms of trade.

- Associated with the Asian model has been, until the mid-1997 shocks, a sense of *hubris* among the favored industries, firms, and individuals. When these favored entities confronted market tests that they could not meet, they (and their foreign lenders) expected additional resources to be forthcoming to bail them out. Whether the shortfall was in an old-line major banking house (e.g., Yamaichi in Japan), or an established *chaebol* (e.g., the Halla group in Korea), or the start-up of questionable new ventures (e.g., Indonesia's "Timor" car), it was expected that some "non-market" (i.e., government) preferment would make up the difference.

- Finally, the Asian model has had a corrosive effect on the societies and polities of the affected countries as a result of the favoritism, exclusivity, and corruption associated with the back-channel and non-transparent processes of decisionmaking underlying the Asian model.

That market-mediated allocations of resources have shortcomings associated with them doesn't imply that the subjectively-mediated ones of the Asian model will not have still greater shortcomings. In fact, the legacy of the Japan model and its Asian variants suggests that their associated shortcomings are enormously greater because they tend to be protected and concealed. Lacking the corrective, mediating responses that market mechanisms and incentives usually provide, the shortcomings accumulate until a breakdown occurs.

If this lesson is heeded, Asia's recovery can be rapid and enduring; if it is not, recovery is more likely to be slow and fitful.

Postaudit

This critique of the Japan-centered model of industrial policy and its shortcomings has gained, rather than lost, relevance and validity since it was written in 1998.

Chapter 21

THE END OF ASIA'S ECONOMIC CRISIS

The much publicized Asian economic "crisis," which began with the collapse of the Thai baht in July 1997, is over! Instead of a situation that was initially and properly characterized as a "crisis"—to which some observers implausibly ascribed responsibility for triggering crises in Russia and Brazil as well—Asia currently displays a wide range of economic performance, problems, and prospects. Asia's collective economic circumstances no longer constitute a "crisis."

This is not to deny or minimize the fact that individual countries within the region still confront serious economic problems, with sharply different prospects for alleviating, let alone solving them. But the collective record is both better and more promising than the "crisis" rhetoric implies.

First, consider the four original "crisis" countries: Thailand, Korea, Indonesia, and Malaysia. Following the mid-1997 collapse of the baht, these countries experienced asset deflations of between 40 and 70 percent (analogous to that of the 1930s in the United States), currency depreciations between 30 and 80 percent, and reversals of annual economic growth from mid to high positive single digits (between 6 percent and 9 percent), to negative rates between high single digits and low double digits (between –15 percent and –6 percent).

A slightly edited version was published in **The Los Angeles Times** *on April 25, 1999 under the title "Asia's Financial Health Upgraded From Guarded to Stable."*

By the second quarter of 1999, Korea and Thailand have turned the corner. Their GDP growth, though still negative, is much less so than in the prior year; by the fourth quarter of 1999, both Korea and Thailand will probably experience positive growth rates. In both countries, foreign direct investment (FDI) has resumed—in Korea, FDI increased by two and one-half times to $2.0 billion in the first quarter of 1999, compared to the same period a year ago. Their foreign exchange reserves have increased—slightly in Thailand, and substantially (doubling) in Korea (to $55 billion). And Korea's international credit rating has been significantly upgraded by the Moody and Standard and Poor's rating organizations.

When hospitals and doctors issue bulletins about the condition of particular patients, their progress is sometimes described as moving from "critical" to "serious." Similarly, the condition of Korea and Thailand can be reasonably characterized as having progressed from "crisis" conditions to simply "difficult" ones.

This certainly does not apply to Indonesia and Malaysia. Both continue to register high negative rates of GDP growth, weak or inconvertible currencies (Indonesia and Malaysia, respectively), and plunging asset values. In both cases, political rather than economic factors predominantly account for the economic quagmire that still engulfs them. Unless and until political stability and a favorable and predictable policy environment is realized, the outlook for Indonesia and Malaysia will remain dismal.

The economies of Japan and China confront serious economic problems that not only differ between them, but also differ enormously from those of the previous group of four. While Japan's and China's economic problems are serious, in neither case is the term "crisis" appropriate.

Japan's problems predate and transcend the mid-1997 "Asian" financial crisis, and indeed these problems have only been marginally affected by that crisis. The Japanese economy has stagnated for most of the 1990s decade, experiencing an average annual growth rate of about 1 percent, and in 1999 a *negative* growth rate of about 2 percent. This is a striking contrast to Japan's record of strong and sustained growth in the previous decade. Japan's deep-seated structural problems include an industrial system that has been driven by considerations of size, market share, and exports, rather than profitability; a banking system pervaded by non-performing loans resulting from this distorted industrial base and associated credit misallocations; and a regulatory system marked by the heavy hand of government limiting free entry and market access both within the Japanese economy and from potentially competitive firms outside it.

In recent work at RAND, which attempts to measure the relative degree of economic "openness" of different economies, the economy of Japan ranks far below those of the United States and Germany, and is roughly similar to China and Korea in the non-tariff barriers to economic openness permeating the economy, and in impeding market access by foreign businesses.

Yet Japan's per capita gross domestic product remains among the highest in the world (about $40,000), and its current account surplus and foreign exchange reserves ($125 billion and $220 billion, respectively) are the world's largest. While most observers believe that Japan's three-pronged reform policies—bailing out the major banks to make their balance sheets more robust, increasing levels of public spending, and providing a modest degree of deregulation—are too little and too timid to deal with the economy's fundamental structural problems, it cannot be said that Japan is in a "crisis" condition.

China, like Japan, has been only marginally affected by the mid-1997 crisis elsewhere in Asia. Its recent economic performance and near-term prospects are decidedly mixed. Among the positive indicators, its GDP growth has been high and sustained. Even allowing for the occasional fuzziness of China's statistics, annual growth has been and currently is between 5 and 7 percent. Its current account surplus has been running at an annual rate of over $30 billion; foreign exchange reserves are about $150 billion (the second largest after those of Japan); and annual foreign direct investment is more than $35 billion—the largest of any emerging market country. Still another of the positive indicators is the progress made in the government's "buy-out" of the military's ownership of many commercial businesses.

To be sure, there is an equally impressive list of negative signs and signals. Hundreds of large state-owned enterprises (SOEs) continue to register negative net earnings, although Zhu Rongji has mandated them to register profits within the next two years or be liquidated. The four major state banks are dominated by non-performing debt that has been perennially accumulated to cover the persistent losses of the SOEs. Yet, the financial system continues to misallocate credit in favor of the inefficient SOEs, while constraining credit access by the more dynamic non-state and emerging private sector. Whether or not China succeeds in becoming a member of the World Trade Organization later this year, the future robustness of China's economic performance will depend on substantial progress in opening its economic and financial markets.

Although China confronts myriad difficult economic problems, they do not qualify as approximating a "crisis."

The final piece in the complex and variegated Asian economic mosaic is the smaller, more resilient economies: Taiwan, Hong Kong, and Singapore. Although they differ from one another—for example, Taiwan and Singapore have floating exchange rate systems, while Hong Kong maintains a fixed-peg currency board—they also have certain similarities. Each has been seriously impacted by the economic reversals elsewhere in the region, Hong Kong most severely by the bursting of its bubble in asset and property prices. Both Singapore and Hong Kong have registered negative GDP growth as a result of these impacts. Still, the three economies have shown an impressive capacity to adapt to changing circumstances, and to maintain (in the case of Taiwan) or to resume significant economic growth in the near future.

Once again, the term "crisis" is inapt: the reality is more buoyant.

It is time to deflate the rhetoric of "economic crisis": it is a distinctly misleading characterization of the widely differentiated, as well as generally *reflating*, Asian economic environment.

Postaudit

In retrospect, I was more optimistic about Asia's economic recovery than the post-1998 record has warranted. Still, deflating the "crisis" rhetoric was legitimate.

Chapter 22

WHEN GOOD NEWS ISN'T NEWSWORTHY

When East Asia experienced sharp economic reversals in 1997–1998, the profusion of media reports used words like "meltdown," "collapse," and "crash." East Asia's recovery in 1999 and 2000 has been no less dramatic, but the rhetoric used to describe it has been both more restrained and less abundant.

This asymmetry has several explanations. One is simply the media's predilection for bad news over good.

A second relates to uncertainty about the robustness of the recovery, and the desire of commentators to avoid being too far out on a limb if the turnaround turns around.

A third explanation is that the 1997–1998 economic shocks jeopardized the balance sheets of money-center banks in the United States, Europe, and Japan. The jeopardy arose because billions of dollars of short-term loans were made in the frenetic 1995–1997 period without adequate attention to the "due diligence" standards which the banks profess, but did not follow in this instance. By 1999, when the Asian recovery was well underway, the banks' predicament had been significantly relieved by the largesse of the IMF and its governmental contributors.

---

*A slightly edited version was published in **The Los Angeles Times** on July 23, 2000 under the title "Have You Heard About the Incredible Journey?"*

There is no question that the economic turmoil, which ensued in East Asia in 1997–1998, was severe. Four Asian economies—Thailand, Korea, Malaysia, and Indonesia—that had realized high positive GDP growth in 1996 experienced *negative* growth between 5 percent and 12 percent in 1997 and 1998. Asset values in these "crisis" countries plummeted by about 75 percent due to the combined effects of currency depreciation, and deflated equity and property valuations. Averaging over the four economies, an asset worth $100 in June was worth only $25 a year later.

By the second quarter of 2000, the turnaround has been extraordinary. Korea, Thailand, and Malaysia currently have annual growth rates equal to or above those of 1996. Indonesia's growth—about 3-4 percent—is surprisingly high as well as shaky because of serious problems and uncertainties which beset it largely unrelated to the 1997–1998 economic turmoil. The problems include civil and military unrest in Timor, Atjeh, and the Moluccas, and the continuingly ambiguous if not portentous position of its military establishment in the country's political future.

Other indicators of the recovery's surprising strength abound. Capital inflows have resumed, mainly in the form of direct investment rather than debt. Korea, which was almost closed to foreign direct investment prior to the turmoil of 1997, received $15.5 billion of FDI in 1999, five times the 1996 inflow. The current accounts of the four economies are positive, and their foreign exchange reserves are above those held in 1996 (except for Indonesia). Their currencies—whose exchange rates are now flexible rather than artificially pegged as they were in 1997— have regained more than 50 percent of their pre-crisis values. Finally, the foreign debt that remains has been substantially restructured in favor of long-term rather than short-term obligations.

The abundant evidence of recovery is all the more impressive because the Japanese economy, which had long been viewed by the conventional unwisdom in the United States and in the International Monetary Fund as the essential engine for East Asia's recovery, continues to stagnate. Japan's deep-seated economic troubles predate and transcend the Asian financial crisis, and have been only marginally affected by it.

Asia's other major economy, China, continues to register significant growth, although still beset by problems which are largely independent of the 1997–1998 crisis: for example, the continuing heavy burden of its subsidized state-owned enterprises, a poorly managed and vulnerable banking sector, and widespread corruption.

Although the East Asian economies are doing remarkably well, this doesn't mean that all their vulnerabilities have been overcome, nor that business cycles have been repealed. Indonesia's serious and still unfolding problems have already been mentioned. Korea's large and amorphous *chaebols* still require reform, as well as explicit non-preferment in their access to credit or other benefactions. In Thailand, one-third of the banking systems' loans are "non-performing." And Malaysia's Mahathir has perhaps only temporarily backed away from his belief that tightly-regulated capital markets are better than less-regulated ones.

Nevertheless, the upward trajectory of the Asian economies is likely to endure because of five lessons—four tactical and one strategic—which appear to have been learned from the debacles of 1997–1998:

As a form of foreign capital inflow, direct investment is far preferable to debt.

- When emerging market countries or corporations borrow abroad they should not borrow short and invest or re-lend long—a pervasive practice leading up to and precipitating the 1997 Asian crisis.

- Borrowing in foreign ("hard") currency and re-lending or investing for purposes that do not generate foreign currency earnings should be avoided, or at least limited by availability of ample foreign exchange reserves.

- Domestic currency shouldn't be pegged to the U.S. dollar, unless fiscal and monetary policies and institutions are strong enough to support the peg.

Finally, in charting development strategy, what used to be referred as the "Japan development model" should be eschewed. The Japan model, much extolled in the 1970s and 1980s, predicated resource allocations on the basis of non-market, industrial-policy preferment for chosen firms or industries, rather than on market criteria of costs and profitability.

While these lessons provide grounds for optimism, there is also a perverse lesson conveyed by the previous financial turmoil and the quick-fix remedies adopted to redress it. Moral hazard is the perverse lesson that may well counter, if not negate, the positive lessons that have been learned. If events turn sour—whether as a consequence of mistaken public policies in emerging market countries, or of the misguided lending practices of banking institutions in the wealthy countries, a belief has been nurtured that IMF or other government bailouts will come to the rescue. The unintended but perverse result may be to encourage irresponsible behavior that can lead to crises in the future. Notwithstanding the hoped-for reform of the International Monetary Fund, its increased financial resources and heightened aspirations may actually intensify the dangers of moral hazard in the future.

Postaudit

The points about foreign lending, direct investment, and especially moral hazard that seemed to me important lessons from the 1997–1998 Asian financial troubles remain valid and relevant.

Chapter 23

ASIA'S DRAMATIC RECOVERY

East Asia's recovery in 1999 and 2000 has been no less dramatic, though much less publicized, than its deep economic reversals in 1997 and 1998.

Triggered by the collapse of Thailand's baht in July 1997, four economies that had high positive GDP growth in 1996 experienced *negative* growth between 5 percent and 12 percent in 1997 and 1998. Asset values in these "crisis" countries—Thailand, Korea, Malaysia, and Indonesia—plummeted by about 75 percent due to the combined effects of currency depreciation and deflated equity and property valuations. Averaging over the four economies, an asset worth $100 in June of 1997 was worth only $25 a year later.

To place these reversals in historic context, recall that the U.S. financial shocks of 1929–1932, 1962, and 1987 witnessed declines in the Standard and Poor's index of 87 percent, 28 percent, and 34 percent respectively.

By the second quarter of 2000, the turnaround of the East Asian economies has been extraordinary. Korea, Thailand, and Malaysia currently have growth rates equal to or above those of 1996. Indonesia's growth—about 5 percent at an annual rate—is surprisingly high as well as profoundly shaky because of myriad problems and uncertainties which bedevil it: civil and military unrest in Timor, Atjeh, and

---

A slightly edited version was published in **The Weekly Standard** *on June 5, 2000 under the same title.*

Ambon, and the continuingly ambiguous position of Indonesia's military establishment.

Other indicators of the recovery's strength abound. Capital inflows have resumed, mainly in the form of direct investment, rather than debt. Korea, for example, which was almost closed to foreign direct investment prior to the turmoil of 1997, received $15.5 billion FDI in 1999, five times the level in 1996. The current accounts of the four economies are now positive, their foreign exchange reserves are above those held in 1996 (except for Indonesia), and their currencies, whose exchange rates are now flexible rather than artificially pegged, have regained 50 percent or more of their pre-crisis values.

The abundant evidence of recovery is all the more impressive because the Japanese economy—long viewed by much of the conventional unwisdom in the U.S. and the International Monetary Fund as the essential engine for East Asia's recovery—continues to stagnate.

Asia's other major economy, China, continues to register significant growth, although beset by problems which are largely independent of the 1997–1998 crises.

Although the East Asian economic picture is roseate, this doesn't mean that there are not serious soft spots, nor that business cycles have been repealed. Indonesia's serious as well as still unfolding problems have already been mentioned. Korea's large and amorphous *chaebols* still require reform, as well as explicit non-preferment in their access to credit or other benefactions. Nevertheless, the upward trajectory of the Asian economies is likely to endure because of five lessons—four tactical and one strategic—which appear to have been learned from the debacles of 1997–1998:

- First, as a form of foreign capital inflow, direct investment is far preferable to debt.

- Second, when foreign borrowing is resorted to, the repayment period should not be shorter than the yield from the uses to which loans are put (don't borrow short and lend long—a pervasive practice leading to the 1997 crisis).

- Third, don't borrow in foreign ("hard") currency and then re-lend or invest for purposes whose yields do not generate foreign currency (at least, don't engage in this practice without ample foreign exchange reserves).

- Fourth, don't peg domestic currency to the U.S. dollar (unless fiscal and monetary policies and institutions are strong enough to support the peg).

Finally, in charting development strategy, eschew what used to be referred to as the "Japan development model," which predicated resource allocations not on the basis of market criteria of costs and returns, but instead on non-market based preferment for particular firms or industries.

Postaudit

This is an abbreviated version of the same story as presented in the previous chapter, so my assessment of it is also the same.

Chapter 24

CHINA AFTER DENG

Most discussions of potential changes within China since Deng Tsiaoping's demise focus on possible political and leadership changes that may ensue in the next several years. Yet these dimensions of China's landscape are probably less prone to change, and more likely to exhibit continuity, than some others.

To be sure, Jiang Zemin did not ascend to the peak of China's hierarchy with nearly as strong prior credentials—notably those relating to close associations and high formal military rank in the PLA—as did Deng and Mao. Nevertheless, this difference can be overdrawn. In the half-dozen years that Jiang has been chairman of the Central Military Commission, he has so enhanced his support among the top military leaders that one among them, General Chi Haotian, China's defense minister, has been quoted as placing Jiang on a par with Deng and Mao in having made "unique contributions to the PLA."

In addition to the strong base Jiang has acquired in the military, his entrenchment in the party is apparently as solid and secure as the arcane world of intramural Chinese politics permits. So, China's political landscape is likely to continue its brand of strong authoritarian, perhaps gradually liberalizing, centralism, led by Jiang as president, party chairman, and chairman of the Central Military Commission.

Major changes within China are therefore more likely to ensue in the next decade in two other dimensions rather than in China's politics

---

*A slightly edited version was published in **The Los Angeles Times** on April 6, 1997 under the title "New Focus on Military Might."*

or leadership, namely, slower economic growth, and rising military spending (especially spending on military procurement and military research and development).

In the past two decades, China's economy has grown at an extraordinarily high average rate of 9–10 percent annually, propelled by the combined effects of market reforms (first in agriculture, then in other sectors), high rates of interest, new industries, and expanded exports. These rates are likely to be reduced by half, during the next decade. (Growth rates between 3 and 6 percent have been estimated in a recently published RAND study covering this period, although it should also be mentioned that forecasts by such other sources as the World Bank have been considerably higher.)

Five principal reasons account for this prospective slowing in China's rate of growth:

First, China's economy has more than doubled in the past decade—it is now the world's second largest—so any specified *percentage* rate of growth requires larger *absolute* increments of GDP. (As a share of GDP, China's rate of investment is likely to decline somewhat because the economy's *marginal* savings rate will probably be less than the 30–35 percent *average* savings rate of the past decade.)

Second, foreign capital inflows, while continuing to be substantial, will probably decline modestly in the future. In recent years, annual long term inflows of private direct, and portfolio investment in China have been about $35–40 billion annually, two-thirds of which have come from "overseas" Chinese, especially overseas Chinese in Taiwan, Hong Kong, and Southeast Asia. This particular source of foreign capital, and the technology and management associated with it, is likely to diminish as alternative, lucrative investment opportunities expand elsewhere in Southeast Asia.

Third, China's policymakers are embarking on a plan to reduce the wide income disparities created by Deng's "socialist market economy" between the rapidly growing coastal provinces and the rural western ones. Statistical studies done by the Chinese Academy of Sciences have highlighted these disparities by quantifying and publishing them. To redress these disparities, or at least to mitigate them, China's fiscal policies will be adapted to transfer wealth from richer urban to poorer rural areas. Whatever the social and political merits of this policy, the result is likely to dampen China's aggregate economic growth if these resource transfers raise consumption rather than investment.

Fourth, resources are likely to be absorbed by the need to reverse, or at least reduce, the environmental damage (notably of urban water supplies, and atmospheric pollution) caused by rapid industrialization, and especially the massive burning of coal. (Whether reform of inefficient state-owned enterprises might free resources to partly offset these rising environmental needs is conceivable, but not likely.)

Finally, China's military spending is likely to rise, to some extent at the expense of the rest of the economy. The 12.7 percent increase in officially announced military outlays for 1997, though commensurate with other governmental expenditure increases, is one indication of this trend.

Besides its effect on economic growth, substantially increased military spending—especially spending on procurement of modern weapons and on military research and development, is likely to be a distinguishing feature of the next decade, compared to the preceding one. Most of China's spending on military equipment and military R&D is financed through the budgets of the cognizant technical ministries (aeronautics and astronautics, marine and shipping, transportation, telecommunications, and the State Commission on Science, Technology, and Industry—COSTIND), rather than the official budget of the defense ministry itself. Consequently, it is generally acknowledged by analysts outside China that the officially reported budget of the defense ministry is only a fraction of total military spending—a characteristic that, incidentally, was derived from and precisely replicates that of the Soviet Union in bygone days.

From the point of view of China's top leaders, significant increases in defense spending should be viewed by the outside world as normal, overdue and non-threatening. Underlying this view is their keen awareness that China has a 10,000 mile land border and 3,000 miles of coastline that warrant enhanced protection against some neighbors that have not always been friendly to China in the past. Moreover, military modernization was fourth on the list of Deng Tsiaoping's well-known "four modernizations" (after agriculture, industry, and technology), and its active pursuit has hitherto been deferred.

Catch-up investment in this form of modernization therefore appears to the leadership as overdue. (That the PLA's influence in the matrix of Chinese politics has increased lends added force to this stance.)

There is a final element that both reinforces these views, and in turn is reinforced by them. In the eyes of China's policymakers, and many of its intellectuals as well, peace and stability in the Asia-Pacific region will be enhanced by a better balance of power among the United States, Japan, and China. Currently, in Chinese eyes, this balance is impaired because China is relatively weak in this triangular relationship. Consequently, strengthening its military power, along with its enhanced economic strength, is viewed as contributing to regional stability, rather than disturbing it.

In sum, the principal changes impending in China in the coming decade are a slower pace of economic growth, and a rising scale of military spending. Fitting China into the global economic environment may be facilitated by the former change. Fitting it into the global security environment may become more difficult and challenging due to the latter one.

China's expanding linkages and engagement in international private investment and trade transactions, as well as its participation in multilateral institutions like the recently initiated G-6 meeting in Tokyo on financial and currency matters, and prospectively in the WTO, can contribute to smoothing China's global economic role. And institutions like the ASEAN Regional Forum (ARF), as well as regularized bilateral and trilateral interactions among China, the United States, and Japan, can facilitate an appropriate role for China in the international security environment.

Postaudit

My forecast that Jiang Zemin's tenure would experience slower growth and rising military spending compared to that of Deng Tsiaoping was on the mark.

Chapter 25

WHY CHINA'S 8 PERCENT GROWTH TARGET IS NOT GOOD NEWS

When senior Chinese economists are asked these days to comment on prospects for continued economic liberalization and reform, they typically respond by addressing a different question: how can China boost its GDP growth to a newly-established target rate of 8 percent annually in 1998 and 1999? Achieving this target is accorded special attention because of the "slowdown" (sic) to 7.2 percent reported in the first quarter of 1998. This response is usually accompanied by emphasizing a massive government infrastructure program of $750 billion to $1 trillion over the next two or three years to assure that the 8 percent goal is reached.

This is not good news for promoting economic liberalization and progress in China. An infrastructure program of such enormous scale, if indeed it were implemented, would preempt for *public* investment more than 40 percent of China's gross investable resources. Private and quasi-private investment (including the so-called "township and village enterprises"), which have been the main engines of China's growth in the past decade, have already been constricted by the predominant share of "policy lending" to state-owned enterprises (SOEs) by the four major state banks. Implementation of an infrastructure-dominated 8 percent growth effort would further squeeze resources available to these non-state businesses.

A slightly edited version was published in **The Wall Street Journal** *on July 21, 1998 under the title "China's Misguided Growth Plan."*

Incidentally, but not insignificantly, such resource reallocations would make depreciation of China's currency more likely because non-state businesses are the main sources (nearly 75 percent) of export earnings, while large scale infrastructure spending would increase demand for imports. This asymmetry would put pressure on the renminbi in China's foreign exchange market.

But this is only part of the bad news. Fixing a target growth rate as the lodestar for guiding development recalls the rigid practices of failed centrally-planned economic systems in the past. It is a detour on the road to a modernized, open, and competitive Chinese economy.

Chinese policymakers respond to such criticisms with two arguments: first, a growth rate of 8 percent is essential to provide jobs for China's high and rising number of urban unemployed; and second, massive infrastructure investments are the most rapid and effective means of reaching this target and generating the necessary employment.

This argument is unconvincing. Most of China's job creation, as well as output expansion, in recent years, have come from non-state enterprises whose share of GDP has risen from one-third in 1985 to over two-thirds currently, while that of the SOEs has fallen correspondingly.

Moreover, while an 8 percent growth target, mainly pursued through public infrastructure investments, would make some inroads on China's unemployment problem, the results would be temporary and still fall far short of remedying the problems. Many of the resulting jobs could well have the character of "make-work" activities, without enhancing productivity in the rest of the economy.

According to the Shanghai Institute of Foreign Trade, 65 percent of China's urban population of 400 million are of working age, between 18 and 60. Estimates of unemployment among this 260 million person workforce range widely, from a low figure of 12 million mentioned by President Jiang Zemin in a recent interview, to other official estimates of 26 million (10 percent of the urban labor force), and much higher numbers that purport to include redundant employment in SOEs, plus regular inflows of peasants from rural areas seeking jobs in cities.

On reasonable assumptions about the relationship between GDP growth and employment, a figure of 8 percent growth would apparently contribute appreciably to job creation, perhaps increasing employment between 12 and 17 million. While these effects would be consequential if they materialize, they would not remedy China's structural unemployment problems. If such increases in employment were achieved through huge infrastructure investments, the resulting employment gains might be apparent and transitory, rather than real and enduring.

Choosing among alternative public works projects typically lacks the benefit of market-based criteria to guide choices. From the standpoint of job creation and recorded growth, building a road from somewhere to nowhere has the same short-term effect as one built from somewhere to somewhere. A newly constructed building with a queue of waiting buyers or leasers has the same effect as one that is nearly bereft of buyers, like the innumerable "see-through" commercial buildings in Pudong and Shenzhen that have created impressive skylines, but are predominantly without occupants.

Moreover, the lack of market-based investment criteria for such an infrastructure program—and rigorous cost-benefit analysis is unlikely to be undertaken to guide project selection if a massive infrastructure program were pursued at a rapid pace—would be an invitation to politically-based choices and to corruption.

This is not to say that China doesn't need major improvements of transportation and other infrastructure facilities. The point is that overreliance on rapid infrastructure expansion to power a specified 8 percent growth target runs a high risk of building monuments rather than soundly-conceived facilities, and of worsening China's unemployment problems in the future by well-intentioned efforts to mitigate them in the present.

To remedy China's formidable unemployment problems in an enduring manner requires continued efforts to liberalize and reform the economy. If China's economic environment can provide ample opportunities for the emergence of thousands of Chinese entrepreneurs—acting alone, or through township and village enterprises, or through joint ventures with foreign investors—then China's real economic growth will be accelerated and job creation will be substantial and enduring.

China's good news is that progress in reform and liberalization continues to flourish. Sustaining it should not be curtailed by or subordinated to the demands of an arbitrary 8 percent growth target and a massive infrastructure investment program geared to reaching it.

Postaudit

Whether because of this essay (unlikely) or in spite of it, China's leaders have lowered their symbolic annual growth target to 7 percent and have become somewhat less fixated on it.

Chapter 26

CHINA'S DEVALUATION: WHETHER, WHEN, HOW MUCH?

Toward the end of each of the past three years, a question has perennially arisen as to whether, when, and by how much China will devalue the yuan. In fact, this is the wrong question.

The right question is, whether and when will China move from a partly convertible to a fully convertible currency, and from a semi-pegged to a flexible exchange rate system? And, by the way, at what exchange rate would a flexible yuan be likely to trade?

What typically precipitates the devaluation question is a shortfall in several economic indicators behind goals previously announced by China's leaders. In the first half of 1999, China's exports and current account surplus decreased by about 9 percent compared to the corresponding period a year earlier. (Never mind that a smaller current account surplus, let alone a current account deficit, may in fact be quite healthy for a rapidly growing economy.) Foreign direct investment also declined by about 10 percent in this same period (at an annual rate of over $35 billion, FDI in China remains by far the largest among all developing countries). GDP growth, while having slowed a bit, has remained creditable, although it is probably one or two percentage points lower than the officially reported figures. Moreover, the economy is troubled by incipient deflation and even potential recession. Consumer prices have fallen by 1–2 percent in

*A slightly edited version was published in **The Asian Wall Street Journal** on October 25, 1999 under the title "Free the Yuan."*

the past year, and demand has weakened, notwithstanding substantial increases in government infrastructure spending.

Despite these and other problems, there are two reasons why the devaluation question as it is usually posed is wrong.

First, the connection between devaluation and the various indicators shortfalls which it is intended to remedy is remote. More than half of China's exports depend on imported inputs. Devaluation would raise the yuan costs of these, as well as other imports. To the extent that the costs of such other imports as grain also rise and lead to increased labor costs, export gains from devaluation would be further reduced. Furthermore, the effects of devaluation would run counter to Beijing's declared aim of reducing the large income disparities between the richer coastal provinces and the poorer central and western ones. The coastal regions, where exports are concentrated, would realize some gains from devaluation because of somewhat lowered yuan costs of exports, whereas the interior provinces would be adversely affected by the increased costs of imported consumer goods. Hence, the disparities between rich and poor would be aggravated.

The effect of devaluation on foreign direct investment is also ambiguous. On the one hand, devaluation would increase the exchange value of foreign funds and their ability to acquire and employ indigenous resources, thereby encouraging capital inflow. On the other hand, devaluation would equivalently reduce the exchange value of profits resulting from such investment, thereby tending to discourage FDI. Moreover, a devaluation now might engender worries that another devaluation would take place later, thereby further discouraging FDI. Devaluation would also tend to weaken China's credit rating for commercial as well as sovereign debt, thus raising the costs of foreign borrowing.

The second, and still more important, reason why the question as usually posed is wrong is that it ignores the key issue of the yuan's inconvertibility on capital account—a significant matter from the standpoint of China's status as a "normal" and major player in the global economy. Both for China and the world economy, it is distinctly less important whether China has an *inconvertible* currency pegged, as it is currently, between 8.2 and 8.3 yuan per U.S. dollar or pegged at a devalued rate of, say, 10.2 per U.S. dollar, than whether the yuan is *fully convertible* while its rate of exchange fluctuates, as does that of the dollar, yen, and euro. Hence, the devaluation question should be framed in terms of whether and when will China move from a partly convertible to a fully convertible currency, and from a semi-pegged to a flexible exchange rate system?

A convincing argument can be made that China is now, or soon will be, in a position to accomplish this major change, in the process generating significant benefits for the economy's next development phase:

- The term structure of China's foreign debt is favorable for convertibility: 80 percent of the debt is long-term.

- Foreign exchange reserves, estimated at $150 billion, are four or five times China's short-term debt. Moreover, the $150 billion figure—an increase of 5 percent from a year ago—is probably underestimated. Since 1997, major exporters have been allowed to retain up to 15 percent of their foreign exchange earnings without recourse to the Central Bank, and at least some of these assets would be available to the central government if necessary.

- Convertibility of the yuan would provide a strong incentive for both direct foreign investment and long-term portfolio investment. To be sure, investors in China, as in other countries, would still face a currency risk, but one that would be more familiar, more manageable, and more hedgeable than that associated with pegged rates (as suggested by the collapse of pegged-rate systems in the 1997–1998 Asian financial crisis).

- Moving toward a convertible, flexible rate system by normalizing the status of China's currency would enhance China's stature in the World Trade Organization, and prospectively as a member of the G-7/8 Group.

- Finally, embracing a fully convertible, flexible rate system would be an invaluable element in furthering China's economic liberalization efforts. At China's relatively low interest rates (3–4 percent), convertibility would be likely to galvanize demand for capital in the entrepreneurial non-state sectors of the domestic economy, as well as boost foreign capital inflows. In the process,

China would become more open to and connected with the global economy.

It is not at all clear where a convertible and flexible yuan would actually trade against the dollar in the near-term and the longer-term future. China's nominal (pegged) exchange rate is between 8.2 and 8.3 yuan to the dollar. Its purchasing power parity rate is at least two to three times that value: between, say, 3 and 4 yuan per dollar. It is as plausible that, with a convertible currency, the nominal exchange rate of the yuan would appreciate as that it would depreciate.

Postaudit

As China continues to boost its foreign exchange reserves (by more than 40 percent since 1999, when this essay was written), the questions of whether and when it may shift to a fully-convertible yuan remain unanswered, as does the question of whether the exchange value would depreciate or appreciate.

Chapter 27

CHINA'S HIERARCHS FACE A CRITICAL DILEMMA

China's socialist market economy is starting to look much more like capitalism, creating a new dilemma for the nation's communist leadership.

In the next few months, mainland China's first free and competitive stock market, known as the second board market, will open. Unlike existing stock exchanges in Shanghai and Shenzhen, whose listings are mainly state-owned, partly privatized companies, the new market's listings will consist largely of private Chinese businesses, many involved in high technology, and joint ventures between Chinese and foreign investors whose companies are registered in China. The Shanghai and Shenzhen stock markets will be consolidated in Shanghai and reconstituted as the first board market, while the new exchange will be based in Shenzhen.

The second board market, or "China's Nasdaq," will stimulate the country's embryonic venture-capital industry and help sort out Chinese entrepreneurs and their start-up companies. It will enable emergent Chinese entrepreneurs to acquire financing from the country's huge supply of domestic savings through issuing stocks in their own companies, thereby further expanding their dominance in the Chinese economy.

To the custodians of Communist orthodoxy, this presents a challenge. True, the party has accepted Deng Xiaoping's permissive dic-

---

*Published in **The Los Angeles Times** on February 11, 2001 under the title "Communist Ideologues Struggle to Make Room for Capitalists."*

tum on market economics: It doesn't matter what the cat's color is, so long as it catches the mice. But some top Communist ideologues believe that the new stock market poses a troubling question: Should the party allow Chinese entrepreneurs to be members?

This is no idle question, as a recent conversation I had in Beijing with one of the Communist Party's top theorists points up.

"State ownership of the principal means of production remains a fundamental tenet of Communist theory, notwithstanding recognition of the important role that markets must play, especially in the early stages of China's development," the theorist said. "So it would be inconsistent and inappropriate to include within the party entrepreneurs who have a fundamentally different belief."

Yet, he readily acknowledged another side to the issue, one that would sacrifice ideology in favor of pragmatism. "If these entrepreneurs are not included inside the party, they will be more inclined to form other groups outside the party, and they will have the resources to do so."

I suggested that the dilemma may resolve itself, since entrepreneurs of start-up businesses typically spend all their waking hours on their businesses. As such, they probably wouldn't want to become party members, let alone have the time to do so.

The theorist corrected me. Workers respect party membership, he said, and that respect raises their productivity. Then he added, "Party members also are likely to have more influence and be more effective in their dealings with government officials than are non-party members."

Both responses are cause for pause, especially the second, since it implies favoritism and perhaps more egregious forms of corruption in the future, despite official pronouncements that the entire system's legitimacy depends on expunging corruption. Indeed, if entrepreneurs were admitted into the Communist Party, thereby ensuring them greater market influence, the party itself, rather than rooting out corruption, might inadvertently promote it.

Short of that, a new entrepreneurial capitalist class inside the Communist Party would markedly push the party in a pluralistic direction, perhaps along the lines of Japan's faction-riven Liberal Democratic party. But if entrepreneurs remain non-members, the party will likely become increasingly remote from, and decreasingly relevant to, developments in the real world.

More broadly speaking, the Chinese Communist Party will either metamorphose along with the economy or it will be eclipsed. The opening of the second board market will move us closer to the answer.

Postaudit

Five months after this essay was published, private businessmen (i.e., "capitalists") were declared eligible for membership in China's Communist Party, but launching of the second board market has been indefinitely deferred.

Chapter 28

COMMUNISTS AND CAPITALISTS IN CHINA: WHO WILL CO-OPT WHOM?

The defining event in China in the first year of the 21st century is probably not the EP-3/F-8 aircraft collision near Hainan and its aftermath, or the detention, trial, and release of Chinese-American scholars, or the repression of the Falun Gong, or the award of the 2008 Olympics to Beijing—although each of these is important. The defining event is the decision of the Chinese leadership to admit acknowledged capitalists to membership in the Communist Party of China (CPC). The ramifications of this decision include the prospect of two very different futures: (1) a "capitalists co-opt party" scenario, or (2) a "party co-opts capitalists" scenario.

At the 80th anniversary of the CPC on July 1, 2001, President Jiang Zemin declared that the CPC should formally accept private business owners (read, "capitalists") as party members. The point was reiterated and reinforced three weeks later by Jiang's announcement that he will propose to the party's Central Committee meeting in late September a change in the party's constitution to allow explicitly for private businessmen to be admitted to party membership.

The new policy is intended to reflect Jiang's personal contribution to communist "theory"—the so-called "Three Representations" doctrine. This element of communist esoterica mandates the party to represent and to promote "advanced productivity," "advanced cul-

*A slightly edited version was published in **The New York Times** on August 13, 2001 under the title "China's Capitalists Join the Party."*

ture," and the "fundamental interests" of China's broad masses, including private businessmen.

While some of this rhetoric is reminiscent of the labyrinths of medieval scholasticism, the bottom line is that clearing the way for capitalists to become party members also clears the way for sharply different futures to emerge in China.

Jiang's pronouncement is the culmination—although perhaps not the end—of a protracted debate within the party's leadership, a debate that has been both stimulated and accelerated by several recent developments in China's economy: a growing proportion of China's gross domestic product (currently probably more than 25 percent) originating in the rapidly-growing private business sector; the continuing progress of privatization of state-owned enterprises; and the planned but postponed launching of a new and genuine stock market for trading private corporate equities. (China's existing stock markets in Shanghai and Shenzhen are anodyne versions of the real thing because more than 75 percent of the voting shares of stocks traded on these markets is owned by the government.) Establishment of the new market, sometimes labeled "China's Nasdaq," is likely to generate a surge of new private companies, IPOs, and capitalist entrepreneurs.

The debate has been protracted because there are strong as well as strongly-held arguments on both sides. Those arguing for exclusion of capitalists from party membership contend that their inclusion would risk further compromising two major pillars of communist ideology: state ownership of the basic means of production (notwithstanding general acknowledgment that markets must play an important role, "especially in the early stages of China's development"), and the doctrine of "classes" and "struggles" between them (in which capitalists traditionally have figured as one of the classes to be struggled against). So, the argument continues, inclusion of capitalists risks further eroding the residue of what's "socialist" in China's slogan of a "socialist market economy."

The evidently compelling argument on the other side is that excluding them from membership carries with it even greater risks. As one senior party theorist said to me, "If these entrepreneurs are not included *inside* the party, they will be inclined to develop organizations and channels *outside* the party, and they will have ample resources to do so." If the capitalists are excluded, the CPC will face a growing gap between itself and the entrepreneurial individuals and groups, whose activities and interactions with the global economy will be further enhanced by China's impending membership in WTO. The CPC would thereby risk becoming increasingly remote from the real world.

Faced with this Hobson's choice between further ideological compromise or increased estrangement from where the action is, the party has opted to accept the former risk in order to reduce the latter one.

With the gateway to party membership open to capitalists, their membership will swell as will their influence within the party. So, who will emerge as dominant? Several scenarios are plausible.

In one scenario, the party will co-opt the capitalists, perhaps in a perverse way that results in still more corruption than that which already pervades the economy and society. One reason why capitalists may choose to join the 65 million present party members is to secure or enhance preferential treatment in their business dealings—including access to credit, property, licenses, contracts, and generally more favorable administrative dispensations. While this "party co-opts capitalists" scenario might aggravate the existing pattern of widespread corruption, it might nonetheless be consonant with continued or even enhanced economic growth—especially if it results in lowering the costs of business transactions through and with government by subjecting them to some sort of party discipline. The "party co-opts" scenario would leave the party's political dominance unimpaired and perhaps even strengthened.

An alternative and more benign "capitalists co-opt party" scenario depends on the fact that "capitalists," rather than being a homogeneous "class," are extremely heterogeneous in China, as elsewhere. Their heterogeneity springs from the compelling differences in what they do and where they do it. They may, for example be high-tech or low-tech, oriented towards external or domestic markets, linked to or distant from foreign capital and technology, pro-WTO and market liberalization or against it, linked with the PLA or averse to it, and so on.

Capitalist entrepreneurs typically have very different, often competitive and frequently conflicting, economic interests. As party members, their divergent interests are likely to be reflected in different groupings, influences, and factions within the party. In the "capitalists co-opt" scenario, these divergent interests will convert the party from a presumption of monolithicity toward an increasing degree of pluralism. Admitting capitalists to party membership may have as its consequences political pluralism, as well as a more dynamic and entrepreneurially-driven economy. Along this road perhaps lies a stronger but more "normal" China.

Postaudit

The dilemma remains unresolved. If I had to place a bet, I would probably guess that, in the mid to long run, capitalists will be the co-optors rather than the co-opted.

Chapter 29

CHINA CONTINUES ITS FITFUL MARCH
TOWARD CAPITALISM

While the Party faithful still refer to China's economic system as a "social market economy with Chinese characteristics," a more apt description is a "mixed state and private economy with *European* characteristics." These characteristics include a pervasive, interventionist government role as producer, regulator, and corporate owner; a growing and innovative private business sector (currently producing more than one-third of China's non-agricultural output); and a variety of joint ventures between government, domestic, and foreign business. (Two of these characteristics also bring to mind the stagnating economy of Japan.)

What Britain's Prime Minister, Tony Blair, has referred to as the "Third Way"—supposedly something between central planning and American-style capitalism—and Germany's Chancellor, Gerhard Schroeder, describes no less elliptically as the "*Neue Mitte*" ("New Middle") embody these mixed attributes which increasingly apply to the Chinese economy, as well.

Two recent developments, in addition to China's admission to the World Trade Organization, indicate the direction in which China's economy is evolving: first, efforts by the China Securities Regulatory Commission (CSRC) to reform China's dysfunctional stock markets; and second, the newly extended welcome to private businessmen to become members of China's ruling Communist Party.

*A slightly edited version was published in **International Economy**, Winter 2002, under the title "Capitalism, Chinese Style."*

153

Bringing Shanghai and Shenzhen stock markets up to speed is one of the principal conditions for sustaining China's high economic growth rate. China has the world's highest savings rate—over 35 percent of annual GDP, compared to less than half that rate in most major economies. Properly functioning security markets help to guide savings into efficient and profitable investments, but this function has not been performed effectively in China. Instead, so-called "policy" loans to state-owned enterprises (SOE's) have been provided by the state-owned banks, in the process preempting capital that could otherwise be available to non-state enterprises through expanded development of the securities markets. As a result, securities markets have been thin and trading volume low. One indicator is the small proportion of GDP represented by the market capitalization of stocks listed on China's markets (by comparison, in the United States the market capitalization of listed stocks is more than 200 percent of U.S. GDP).

To expand and improve the operation of securities markets, the CSRC (China's counterpart to the Securities and Exchange Commission) confronts two major problems: continued government holdings of two-thirds of the voting shares of the "privatized" former SOEs among the 1,100 companies listed on China's exchanges; and the failure of corporate governance of the listed companies to contribute to improving the functioning of equity markets.

To remedy these deficiencies, the CSRC has made several important market-oriented reforms.

First, government holdings are being gradually reduced, although the pace has been constrained by a fear of destabilizing the markets if the pace were accelerated. This dilemma—rapidly reducing government holdings, without unduly destabilizing the markets—is perhaps more tractable than has been assumed. For example, a portion of the government shares might be converted to non-voting preferred stock and transferred to the state banks, thereby offsetting some of the non-performing loans on their fragile balance sheets, while at the same time excluding the government from intervention in corporate management.

Second, the CSRC has been encouraging the listing of new non-state companies, adding about 100 new listings annually—a rate that should be accelerated if and as new companies are able to meet the financial and other standards set by CSRC for initial public offerings (IPOs).

Third, the CSRC has been making serious efforts to educate corporate management, as well as both government and retail shareholders, about the central importance of improving corporate governance to enable securities markets to function more effectively.

Improved corporate governance is essential to make management accountable to prospective shareholders, and thereby to motivate savers and investors to acquire securities, thus widening and deepening the markets. This requires increased transparency in corporate management, frequent and regular financial reporting in accord with rigorous accounting standards, and independent members of corporate boards, audit committees, nominating committees, and compensation committees. These practices are far removed from the typical and familiar practices of business management in China. Where ownership remains predominantly in the hands of the ministry of finance and other government ministries that hold majority shares in listed companies, management remains beholden to government entities, and the interests of *retail* shareholders are largely ignored. Maximizing shareholder value is typically not high among the objectives of government owners.

Another indicator of China's circuitous path toward a more market-oriented system is Jiang Zemin's decision on July 1, 2001 to open the doors for new entrepreneurs to become Party members. Prior to this decision, several thousand businessmen were already among the Party's 65 million members. However, most of them became members while previously employed by the state—for example, by SOEs, by state ministries, or by the military. The July 1 decision anoints "new" capitalists as potentially acceptable party members, thereby overriding the deeply-engrained ideological stance against the profit-oriented business "class," which was previously viewed as something to be resisted rather than embraced.

In the short run, Jiang's decision is no less significant as a symbol than as an operationally significant reflection of accelerated market-oriented reform. Probably the number of capitalists admitted to party membership in the next year or two will be relatively limited in order to forestall opposition by "leftists" in the Party to this "anointment" of capitalists. However, in the middle to longer run, the pace will quicken, and capitalist membership in the Party will swell along with the burgeoning of private business in the Chinese economy. Hence, the policy influence of the business sector is likely to increase significantly in the future. One consequence will be greater pressure to strengthen the rule of law as a precondition for economic performance and for the growth of the business sector. Another consequence is likely to be enhanced pluralism within Party councils reflecting the diversity of business interests across a wide range of economic and regulatory policies and practices.

The vector of near-term and longer-term changes underway in China's economy suggests something more like the mixed system of Europe's "New Middle" economies, rather than a prototypical American system. To be sure, the economic performance of the European economies has been something less than lustrous, and it is at least debatable whether the expanding reach of the European Union's bureaucracy is more likely to improve than to impair it. But in China the prospect that a mixed system involving both government intervention and private capitalism will enhance economic performance may be brighter. Unlike Europe, China's economic system is moving away from the heavy hand of centralized state planning toward a system marked by greater openness, competitiveness, and flexibility.

Postaudit

This chapter's central argument is that China's sustained economic growth will depend significantly on the extent to which its equity markets are able to function as efficient allocators of China's huge pool of aggregate savings. The issue remains important as well as unresolved.

Chapter 30

ONE CHINA, *THREE* SYSTEMS?

One of the striking, as well as neglected, aspects of the recent financial turmoil in Asia is the sharply different impact it has had on the
three China domains: China Mainland, China Hong Kong, and China
Taiwan (the latter, incidentally, is the formal name under which Taiwan registers as a member of APEC). Taiwan, despite its open markets, has maintained a remarkable degree of financial stability in the
midst of the region's turbulence. Hong Kong, notwithstanding its
open markets and a monetary system pegged to the U.S. dollar, has
been acutely volatile. China Mainland, by contrast, has displayed
evident stability by restricted access to and exit from its capital markets.

So striking are the contrasts that it may be timely to replace the standard "one China, two systems" mantra with "one China, *three*
systems," instead! Taiwan's notable ability to reconcile economic
openness with financial stability may also provide some experience
that should be useful to China Mainland as it charts its economic
directions for the future.

Several salient financial indicators highlight the contrast among the
three systems. On a year-over-year basis, in their respective own-
currencies, Hong Kong's stock index showed a decline in market
value of 25 percent, while China's restricted Shanghai and Shenzhen
indexes ("restricted" in both access to and exit by foreign capital, as a
result of regulatory controls as well as non-convertibility of renminbi

---

*A slighted edited version was published in **The Wall Street Journal** on December 18,
1997 under the title "Now It's One China, Three Systems."*

capital assets), showed *gains* of about 30 percent, and Taiwan's open market showed a gain of 11 percent.

The rise and fall of Hong Kong's Hang Seng index in 1997 has been heavily influenced by the so-called "Red Chip" stocks—Hong Kong companies with headquarters in the Mainland or close links to Mainland entities such as the CITIC (China International Trust and Investment Corporation) conglomerates whose parent company in Beijing is a state-owned entity. Prior to Hong Kong's formal reversion to China on July 1, 1997, these Red Chips sparked a bull market based on expectations that they'd receive both capital infusions and preferential market access from Beijing. The Hong Kong financial market reversed course following the transfer of sovereignty, when the magnitude and pace of support from China Mainland turned out to be less than the bulls had expected.

In considerable measure, the instability of Hong Kong's financial market has been due to the presumed, although perhaps exaggerated, influence on the Hong Kong economy exerted, or expected to be exerted, by Beijing.

Taiwan, by contrast, has been relatively insulated from and unaffected by both the pre-reversion Hong Kong "bubble" (especially in real estate and equity markets), and its post-reversion bursting. Of course, Taiwan is and will be significantly influenced by developments both in China and Hong Kong, as well as in the Asian region more generally. Nevertheless the fact that Taiwan has been obliged (in part for political reasons) to maintain a degree of economic distance from its Asian neighbors, and to develop other trade and capital markets as well, has ironically redounded to its advantage in the midst of the region's recent financial turmoil.

Another indicator of the difference and distance between Taiwan's economic system, and those of China Mainland and Hong Kong, is provided by the contrasting behavior of their respective foreign exchange reserves, current account balances, and exchange rates.

Between 1996 and 1997, China's foreign reserves swelled by nearly 40 percent (to $132 billion), those of Hong Kong rose by 55 percent (to $85 billion), while Taiwan's reserves rose only 2 percent (to $88 billion). (China, Taiwan, and Hong Kong ranked in that order, after

Japan, as the largest holders of foreign reserves in the world economy.)

While both China and Hong Kong were boosting their reserves substantially, Taiwan was using its current account surplus to make direct investments outside as well as inside the Asian regions.

The current account balances of the three domains also show different patterns: Hong Kong's current account was in deficit by about $3 billion, while the current account balances of China and Taiwan showed surpluses of $7.2 billion and $9.7 billion, respectively. In the same period, Hong Kong's exchange rate, firmly pegged to the U.S. dollar through its monetary board, remained stable, that of Taiwan depreciated about 15 percent relative to the U.S. dollar, and China's renminbi remained stable but without convertibility on capital account.

Still a further contrast is provided by the pattern of capital flows in the three instances. Long-term capital flows into China year-over-year were over $30 billion, those into Hong Kong were $32 billion, while Taiwan actually realized an outflow of nearly $8 billion, representing its foreign investments, including those in China, Hong Kong, and the United States.

Underlying and contributing to these markedly different patterns among Taiwan, China Mainland, and China Hong Kong are several other significant differences in their respective economic policies and circumstances. Again, on a year-over-year basis, in 1997 the broad money supply (M2, covering demand, savings, and time deposits) increased by 127 percent in China, 114 percent in Hong Kong, and only 10 percent in Taiwan. Inflation rates in China and Hong Kong were similar to one another, 5.2 percent and 5.5 percent respectively, while in Taiwan the consumer price index increased only six-tenths of 1 percent in the same time period.

In sum, the relative financial stability displayed thus far by Taiwan has been the result of evidently cautious macroeconomic policies, especially monetary policy, combined with the acquisition of foreign assets through long-term investments in Asia and elsewhere. By contrast, the monetary policies of both China and Hong Kong have been more expansionary under the influence of substantial inflows of foreign capital, resulting in both instances in somewhat higher inflationary pressures and price increases than those experienced by Taiwan.

The economic differences between Hong Kong and Taiwan are not inconsiderable, although perhaps no greater than those between the disparate members of Europe's prospective Monetary Union. But the economic differences between China and both Hong Kong and Taiwan are much greater. For the vision of "one China" to become practicable, China's economic system will probably have to move much closer to that of Taiwan.

Postaudit

The continued sharp diversity of economic performance among the three entities since this article was written attests to the validity of the central point. Still, the political relevance of these systemic economic differences has probably diminished.

Chapter 31

RESTARTING CROSS-STRAIT RELATIONS: BEYOND THE DIALOGUE OF THE DEAF
(Co-authored with Jonathan Pollack)

The election of Chen Shui-bian as Taiwan's new president and the prospective entry of both China and Taiwan into the World Trade Organization offer a rare opportunity for a fresh start in cross-Strait relations. For the first time since the 1993 agreement in Singapore between designated representatives of the two governments, there is now a possibility that both sides might agree on terms of reference in cross-Strait ties for which neither claims outright ownership or a monopoly of political virtue.

Explicit economic agreements and regulations constitute the common ground where the two sides could break the stalemate in cross-Strait ties and move from intimations of flexibility to tangible results. Such accords would provide significant benefits to both sides, as well as compelling incentives for their continued political and military restraint.

Toward this end, we offer the following ideas for consideration by the two sides as a way of reviving and injecting momentum into their discussions of cross-Strait ties. Befitting Chinese practice, we characterize these initiatives as the "four nows and one soon."

A slightly edited version was published in **The Asian Wall Street Journal** *on May 19–21, 2000 under the title "A New Beginning."*

First, Taipei has long prevented direct investment projects on the mainland larger than $50 million, and has denied any transactions entailing high-technology transfer. In addition, it has consistently precluded, contrary to Beijing's wishes, the establishment of direct air and sea transport across the Taiwan Strait. Taiwan should immediately place these items on the table for discussion.

Second, joint or sequential admission of China and Taiwan into the WTO (with Taiwan joining as a "customs state") can be accompanied or preceded by negotiations on matters of mutual economic interest. These subjects include foreign direct investment, protection of property rights, affirming and implementing the rule of law, technology transfer agreements, and facilitating establishment of joint ventures between firms in China and Taiwan.

Third, both sides should explore their overlapping interests and the mutual gains to be realized by coordinating their respective policies toward development and exploitation of energy resources in the South China Sea.

Fourth, both sides should consider whether these issues on which they have common interests—perhaps sometimes at variance with the interests of other countries in and out of the region—warrant their establishing mechanisms for bilateral consultation and coordination. Such mechanisms could be useful before and during future meetings of the WTO as well as the Asia-Pacific Economic Cooperation (APEC) forum, in which both China and Taiwan are members.

To these four "nows," we would add a fifth "soon." China and Taiwan should be prepared to discuss the perverse interaction between China's development and deployment of missiles that Taiwan views as threatening, and Taiwan's repeated requests to the United States for enhanced air and missile defense systems to counter this threat. Both sides might recognize the prospect of mutual benefits by parallel restraint in this domain. This sensitive issue may not be appropriate to broach immediately, but as soon as signs of progress materialize in less contentious areas.

President-elect Chen clearly seems amenable to exploring these possibilities. He has demonstrated extraordinary discipline and political restraint in the month since his election, studiously avoiding actions or statements that he knows will incur Beijing's wrath. But there is an imperative need to provide more of a structure for cross-Strait ties. A denser and direct web of economic linkages would help provide the ballast and underpinning that these relations presently lack.

It still remains uncertain whether the Chinese see opportunity or danger in Chen's election—or perhaps some of both. Leaders in Beijing did not fully anticipate, let alone prepare for, Chen's victory or the humbling of the Kuomintang, which held sway over the island's politics for more than a half century. Instead, they made rhetorical efforts, which were both conspicuous and ineffectual, to prevent such an electoral outcome. Beijing's leaders remain exceedingly wary of the Democratic Progressive Party, which has long advocated Taiwan's formal independence from the mainland.

But Chen's acute awareness of Beijing's sensibilities, and his restrained comments since his electoral victory, have contributed to a mood of guarded optimism. He has stated his readiness to discuss the "one China" concept, perhaps under a confederal formula. He has also reassured Beijing that (absent the use of force against Taiwan) he will not take any actions that China would deem moves toward a formal declaration of independence. In addition, he has explicitly endorsed China's entry into the WTO and Congressional approval of Permanent Normal Trade Relations status for Beijing.

To be sure, initiatives such as the "four nows and one soon" constitute only one component of a larger accommodation. But an expanded framework for trade and investment would help circumvent the political liabilities that have foreclosed movement in the past. Moreover, prompt initiation of cross-Strait discussions along the lines we suggest would probably shelve any further action on the Taiwan Security Enhancement Act by the United States Senate—an outcome China clearly seeks.

We recognize the political obstacles that could easily doom forward movement. But the two sides now have an unparalleled opportunity to define a mutually acceptable framework that defers the more contentious issues while providing both with tangible economic and political gains. These are matters that China and Taiwan need to pursue in earnest, lest the propitious moment be lost, and stalemate or worse resume.

Postaudit

The "four nows and one soon" agenda that Jonathan Pollack and I proposed remains valid and relevant. The first "now" has been largely realized without formal resumption of cross-Strait negotiations.

Chapter 32

CURING JAPAN'S ECONOMIC MALAISE

For Japan to emerge from its severe and protracted economic doldrums nothing will help as much as abandoning its deep-seated commitment to an export-led economic strategy. Toward this end, Japan should remove the pervasively preferential treatment favoring its export firms and industries, and protecting them, along with domestic industries, from potentially competitive imports.

Japan's export-led strategy should be replaced by an "import-accommodating" one, which would not only benefit Japan but would contribute significantly to the economic recovery of the entire Asian region, as well.

This prescription is heretical. According to standard economic analysis, imports are deflationary while exports are expansionary. For an economy afflicted by recession like that of Japan, export promotion rather than import accommodation is a more conventional therapy. But in Japan, where export-led growth has been a long-standing creed, reversing this course would be salutary because it would open domestic markets and remove the shackles and distortions imposed on the economy by the export-led doctrine.

Sometimes the distortions introduced by export promotion operate through direct measures—for example, through exporters' preferential access to bank credits, or through rebating of taxes on export sales, as distinct from domestic sales. Sometimes the distortions are

---

*A slightly edited version was published in **The Wall Street Journal** on May 20, 1998 under the title "Japan Can't Export Its Way to Prosperity."*

indirect—for example, central bank sales of Japanese yen and the rhetorical flourishes of the *éminence grise* of Japan's economic policies, the Vice Minister of Finance, Eisuke Sakakibara—designed to weaken the yen and thereby strengthen the competitive position of Japanese exports.

Similarly, protection from import competition is sometimes provided by direct measures—for example, import quotas and tariffs. More often, protection is provided by labyrinthine regulatory restrictions in the form of non-tariff barriers—for example, exacting, changeable, and arbitrary customs procedures, standards for inspecting, testing, certifying, and approving import products, restrictions on entry of foreign firms into particular industries and on bidding by foreign firms for government contracts. In recent RAND research on the relative difficulty of doing export business in various foreign countries, a survey of several hundred key business executives in international firms found that Japan's non-tariff barriers make it more difficult doing business there than in the United States, Europe or South Korea, and about as difficult as in China.

Whether by direct or indirect means, and whether the means are designed to promote exports or restrict imports, Japan's perennial pursuit of export-led growth accounts for many of the structural imbalances in its economy. One consequence is the continued amassing of large current account surpluses on top of its already excessive holdings of over $220 billion of foreign currency reserves (three times those of Germany, and about two-thirds as large as those of all fifteen members of the European Union!).

During the past three decades, "export-led growth" (ELG) has been the mantra of development economics. In the 1960s, the underlying theory was that competition in export markets would contribute to improved efficiency and higher quality of export production and, over time, of production for domestic markets as well. In the policy domain, ELG has typically meant preferential attention to and emphasis on promoting exports as a means of boosting economic growth. The formerly-extolled "Japanese development model," emulated and extended in Asia and elsewhere as the "Asian development model," has had as its core principle both the nurturing of export industries, and their protection from import competition in domestic markets. Until the bloom wore off this rosy model in the summer of

1997, ELG had registered significant accomplishments, not only in Japan but among the emulators—notably Korea, Malaysia, and Indonesia, as well. But the doctrine has also had many perverse consequences, which have contributed to Japan's own financial crisis, as well as that of the Asian region.

Export-led growth has several conspicuous flaws:

- The mercantilist mindset underlying it views exports as "good" and imports as "bad." This accords neither with economic sense, nor with common sense. Properly viewed, exports are the lowest-cost means of paying for imports, while it is imports that provide real resources to boost investment and consumption.

- ELG, in its Japanese form and that of its other Asian variants, has created structural imbalances and allocative distortions that impair efficient use of resources. Exports have received favored treatment at the expense of domestic producers and consumers. One result has been to create enormous excess capacity in Japan's steel, cars, chemicals, semiconductor, rubber products, and other export industries.

- The ELG doctrine is, in practice, inextricably associated with the belief that exports should appreciably exceed imports—more broadly, that a country following this policy should register a surplus in its current account. This belief is, as a general rule, logically flawed: everyone's exports can't exceed imports, everyone can't have a current account surplus! Someone has to import and, in the aggregate, current account surpluses somewhere must be balanced by current account deficits elsewhere.

- For Japan to continue accumulating a large current account surplus, when elsewhere in Asia there is a compelling need to provide liquidity and service debt by selling exports to Japan, is anomalous and sharply counterproductive for Asia's economic recovery.

Even in the midst of recent Japanese rhetoric and policy pronouncements about economic stimulus, deregulation, and liberalization, the Japanese policy triangle—bureaucracy, business leadership, and political establishment—is only willing to endorse reforms that minimize challenges to the export-led growth doctrine. So, for example, the most recently publicized stimulus package of $128 billion emphasizes government spending on infrastructure and construction that will largely if not entirely exclude contracts for foreign firms. Tax relief for consumers is relatively small (less than one-quarter of the stimulus package) as well as temporary, thereby assuring that most if not all of the concession will contribute to increased savings rather than consumer spending. To be sure, there is new talk of "deregulation" and "liberalization" associated with the stimulus package. But these measures do not involve removal of non-tariff barriers, or opening of domestic markets to imports; they simply allow some opening of Japan's financial markets to foreign providers of financial services—a welcome change, but one that is likely to help rather than hinder Japanese exports.

It is time—indeed it is well past time—for Japan to acknowledge the flaws in its export-led growth strategy, and to replace it with an "import-accommodating" strategy. This would focus on macroeconomic and microeconomic policies that would be neutral with respect to exports and imports, neither favoring the one nor inhibiting the other. Japan's leadership—and especially its sophisticated bureaucracy—should design an import-accommodating growth strategy to include the following elements:

- Rapid reduction, leading to removal, of all forms of preferential treatment of export firms and industries, and of non-tariff barriers that inhibit import competition.

- Permanent reductions of individual and corporate income taxes to levels that are at or below those in the United States and other successfully-growing developed economies, as well as permanently removing the consumption tax on domestic sales that was initiated several years ago; in conjunction with the preceding point, domestic demand for imports will rise, economic growth will resume, and the tax base will expand.

- Planning for a current account deficit over the next five years that would aim to draw down Japan's excess foreign exchange reserves by at least $50 billion to a more than ample level of $170 billion.

This is admittedly a tall order. From the standpoint of reversing Japan's economic doldrums, and especially those of its neighbors, it is long overdue.

Postaudit

The drawbacks of Japan's pervasive and protracted mercantilist policies are even more evident now than when this was written in 1998. And the recommendations made in the article for reversing Japan's stagnation remain relevant as well as ignored. For example, instead of drawing down its large foreign exchange reserves, Japan has more than doubled them since 1998.

Chapter 33

LONG-TERM PROSPECTS FOR JAPAN

Q: Could we begin with a description of your recent research and how it evolved?

A: In collaboration with three RAND colleagues, I recently worked on economic trends in the People's Republic of China, India, Indonesia, Japan and South Korea, a project funded jointly by the Department of Defense and the Smith Richardson Foundation. This study basically revisited work done in 1989 and 1995 for the Office of the Secretary of Defense that involved examining economic trends and associated military spending and investment in a wide range of countries, some European, some Middle Eastern, and some Asian. In 1994 and 1995, we deepened the research for a subset of those countries to complete a study that has been updated in the last year and a half.

The East Asian financial and economic crisis of 1997–1999 was the motive to go back and see how, if at all, the estimates might change. In the process, we used more recent and better data and amplified the model—which was a standard Cobb-Douglas-Solow aggregate model—for one country at a time. We examined the key parameters of the model by looking at their means for the 10 years before the 1997–1999 turmoil and the variances around those means.

Then, we generally used the means or made some explicit judgmental modifications in such key parameters as rates of growth of capital

*Interview with the author conducted by Dr. Douglas Ostrom of the **Japan Economic Institute** and published by the Institute on July 7, 2000.*

stock, employment, total factor productivity, military spending in relation to gross domestic product, and military investment (consisting of procurement and construction) in relation to military spending. In short, we examined the key parameters over time, made several judgment calls about them for the future, and did some crude sensitivity testing of the effects of changes in the parameters on the results.

This particular methodology has the advantage of being both transparent and simple. If, for example, you conclude that Wolf and colleagues were off on factor productivity in Japan for whatever reason—and you might very well be more accurate in that judgment than we were—you can make that change and it's fairly easy to see what the effects are. That is a big advantage over more elaborate models where you're not sure what's going on.

Q: What factors did you estimate?

A: We derived estimates of GDP and growth rates of per capita GDP, military spending, and the military capital stock, which represents the accumulation of annual investment less depreciation. We made the arbitrary assumption that military procurement for the years up to and including 1994 would have depreciation rate of 10 percent a year and that after 1994, the rate would be 8 percent.

Those figures might have been too high, but the rationale was that systems purchased earlier would be more likely to obsolesce and depreciate faster than those procured more recently. The decision as to whether that difference is 10 percent and 8 percent, or 8 percent and 6 percent, or 6 percent and 3 percent is quite arbitrary. However, it wouldn't have much of an effect on the comparisons among the five countries—China, India, Indonesia, Japan, and South Korea.

We used a three-equation model in which GDP was the dependent variable in the first equation. The independent variables were the ones I mentioned. In the second equation, the dependent variable was military spending and the independent variable was GDP with a parameter reflecting the mean and variance of that for Japan and, separately, for the other four countries. In the third equation, the dependent variable was military capital stock in period t, determined by military capital in $t-1$, plus the share of military spending devoted to military procurement in period t, minus the depreciation of military capital stock in $t–1$.

Q: Where does the study stand now?

A: The study is complete, has been refereed and revised, and now is in the final stages of editing.

Q: How does Japan come out?

A: I am still somewhat bearish about the adequacy and the pace of Japan's liberalization, regulatory reform, opening and so forth, but this isn't a binary kind of thing. The question is where between zero and one you place progress on all of these points—the opening of financial services and of Japanese markets generally, for example. Regardless, the pace is quite modest, it seems to me. In looking at the data for Japan over the studied 10 years, I was stuck, among other things, by the decreasing proportion of new investment that is private and the increasing proportion that represents infrastructure and public investment.

But it's not the proportionality between the two that is striking. If you use a crude Cobb-Douglas-Solow framework and the growth of the civilian capital stock as one of the key parts of the estimated equation, Japan's output and total factor productivity growth look remarkably low over the 1987–1996 period. Therefore, some judgment must be made about what will happen to the rate of growth of the capital stock and, within that, the proportions of public and private capital formation as well as to factor productivity growth. In the latter part of the 10-year period, factor productivity growth actually was negative. Presumably, the effects of completed and ongoing changes will turn that around—but slowly.

Q: Was excessive capital stock accumulation a cause of the negative productivity growth?

A: Capital accumulation is higher than it was. That generates low or negative factor productivity, basically because inputs are growing faster than outputs. You have to make some assessment of how that will change. This is a judgment call about the extent to which the reforms that have been undertaken—financial, marketization, ease of entry and so forth—will affect the distribution of capital formation between the public and private sectors and how factor productivity will be impacted in turn. Our estimates regarding total factor productivity are positive but modest. When we put all of this together, we got an annual compound rate of GDP growth that goes from about 1.2 percent to 1.6 percent in the years from 2000 to 2015.

Q: The 1990s have been called Japan's "lost decade." In the final analysis, its abysmal economic performance was based on the low productivity growth that you described. Why was it so low? Japan's productivity growth was low relative to the other countries in your study as well as its own record. Why?

A: I'm not sure that I know. Perhaps it was an accumulation of influences on resource allocation that resulted from industrial policy or other priorities, or from criteria other than those relating to profitability considerations. I think that there was an overemphasis on capacity development in export industries and in heavy industries, although the automotive industry has been reasonably successful. In addition, Japan's pattern of investment has shown less flexibility and responsiveness to market indicators and market signals than has that of the United States.

Q: Are you saying that Japanese companies already had bad habits or developed them?

A: I think that they developed bad habits that were nurtured by counterproductive and offsetting industrial policies.

Q: These kinds of behavior have persisted into what is a new world?

A: I'm not saying that habits remain the same in Japan but, rather, that the rate of change has been slower than in the United States, for example. Japan has been more rigid, more inert and more resistant to change. There are indirect indicators in the quite remarkable pace of mergers and acquisitions, for instance—and not just foreign M&As but domestic ones as well.

I have written on the relative importance of the World Trade Organization and corporate mergers in the new business environment. In terms of so-called globalization and liberalization, the influence and importance of the WTO has been somewhat exaggerated by both its proponents and opponents. More of the action underway in terms of liberalization and market-opening is through transborder M&As. I think that in the context of our discussion, the pace of M&As—not only transborder but in Japan—is a significant indicator that perhaps too little attention has been devoted to changing the old bad habits.

Q: How does that work?

A: As a general rule, if one company's habits are worse than those of another firm in a related field, the latter acquires the former. The company formed by the merger would show more responsiveness, adroitness, and flexibility with the merged assets and would be more productive.

Q: That's what we hope is happening in the automotive industry where, for example, there is participation by Renault S.A. and, to a more limited degree, by Daimler Chrysler AG?

A: Yes, that's the hope. I think that the liberalization of financial services will have a further effect—probably in the same direction.

Q: In that regard, the Japanese banking industry is involved in some really huge mergers. Twelve of the largest banks have announced merger agreements that, when completed, will result in four superbanks. Is this part of the process? Or is it, as some have speculated, actually the reverse—a "circling the wagons" kind of strategy. In that view, there is no economic rationale for what already are some of the world's largest banks merging to form still-bigger institutions. These experts note the many cultural and other difficulties in Japanese M&As, particularly those involving financial institutions, and conclude that the only reason banks are combining is because they hope somehow to prevent new entries and a more competitive marketplace.

A: Before I answered that question, I'd want to look at the balance sheets of the merged institutions, know who the dominant partner in the merger is and whether the asset portfolio of that dominant partner showed better behavior than the bad habits to which you referred.

Q: In this case, I think that the merging banks are pretty much in the same boat.

A: I'd want to look carefully at that, and I haven't. But basically the question is whether patterns of investment that can be characterized as bad behavior or the result of rigid habits are changing and, if so, at what pace. In general, the acquiring firm sees some opportunities for deriving more value from the assets being acquired than the holder of those assets has been able to exploit. To the extent that this is the underlying rational that generally applies in M&A deals, one would anticipate some improvement in subsequent capital formation. The initial rationale for acquiring a firm's assets and paying something more than the firm's market capitalization is based on the buyer's conclusion that it can do with the assets what the acquired firm hasn't been able to do, either immediately or over time. I think that in itself is a harbinger of better habits.

Again, it's a question of the pace at which this happens. I am not saying that M&As are the only gauge of reform, flexibility and innovation, but, certainly, they are one indicator.

Q: What is the impact of mergers on productivity growth as incorporated, for example, in your model?

A: In my opinion, they are a positive development and a relatively rapid one. While it's not enough to change the estimate of the total factor productivity from slightly negative to hugely positive, it does have some positive effect.

Q: Part of what you are saying is that the need for mergers may result from past government mistakes—industrial policy of various sorts. Another way to deal with that would be to correct the mistakes directly—in other words, end not just explicit industrial policy but other forms of government intervention in the economy that impede innovation and lower productivity.

A: I've focused on M&As because they are obvious. I don't know which indicator is the right one for basing an inference about the pace at which the internal bureaucratization and the layering of regulatory rigidities is relaxing. There is the danger of looking for the key where the light is rather than where the key fell. We probably give more attention to M&As because they are visible. If you have or could find something about the pace at which regulatory overloads are decreasing or regulations are becoming more flexible, more permeable or whatever—which I haven't yet been able to find—that would be terrific.

Q: Another argument implies that regulatory reform is inevitable even without the active support of either Tokyo or corporate Japan. In this view, Japanese companies are quite happy with traditional business practices—permanent employment, to name one. But, at the end of the day, neither government nor industry has any choice. Japan is, after all, primarily a market economy, driven by market forces and profitability. Once companies have to meet a profitability test, they no longer have the luxury of continuing practices like lifetime employment.

A: I would add that government policy now may be less able to provide a cushion through something like debt restructuring for firms unwilling or unable to earn a competitive rate of return.

Q: In the financial sector, one issue has been that large banks, including those that have announced mergers, basically have run out of capital and cannot play their traditional role in creating money. Of concern from a macroeconomic standpoint is the fact that their role in the transmission of monetary policy has been broken.

A: Their ability to absorb the costs of moral hazard created by wayward firms is diminished.

Q: True, but they have problems even providing credit to healthy firms on a market basis because they have written off loans or have made too many bad loans in the past. The government has pumped trillions of yen into the banking system to recapitalize big banks so that they can reenter the market. The question then arises whether this is a kind of de facto coddling of banks on the part of the government.

A: It depends on whether banks revert to previous behavior or whether they discriminate among uncompetitive firms and treat them unequally. For instance, do they use reasonably rigorous lending criteria to determine that a fifth potential borrower has better credit prospects and should have lower loan rate than the previous four companies that applied?

Q: But if the government is standing in the background with more cash to recapitalize banks, all five borrowers may end up being treated equally, even though they shouldn't be.

A: Exactly. Again, it's not all one way or the other. I would think the assurance that the government is standing behind the equal treatment of the worst of the poor credit risks may be less now than it was in the past. What we found in our study was some improvement, but it was not dramatic.

Q: Do you mean improvement compared with the late 1990s?

A: Yes, especially compared to the last five years. The average growth rate in the 1990s was around 1 percent, maybe a little lower in some years and higher in others but not much.

Q: But we are not going to see a cover story on the Japanese economy in *Time* magazine again.

A: No, not like in the roaring 1980s. And such people as James Fallows, Chalmers Johnson, Clyde Prestowitz and Karel van Wolferen who talked about Japan buying America and the like should stand up and be counted as having been wrong.

Q: In the international context, how do Japan's prospects compare with those of China?

A: It depends on whether you use nominal exchange rates or purchasing power parity rates since the latter has the effect of reducing Japan's per capita GDP. Over the next 15 years, Japan still will have a very high level of per capita GDP relative to all Asian countries, even with a 1.5 percent annual growth rate, because its population is stagnant or diminishing. China's yearly growth rate in our calculations turns out to be something like 5 percent to 5.5 percent in the relatively rosy scenario and about half that in the disruptive-growth scenario. If the Chinese do well and if the impact of this success on the pace of military modernization is significant—and our calculations show that it will be significant—that source of worry may be an exogenous stimulus that motivates the Japanese to do something dramatically faster in terms of regulatory reform than they have shown evidence of doing so far.

Q: How would that play out in Japan?

A: I think Japan would feel that it needed more growth than 1 percent—say, 3 percent a year. But to get to 3 percent, Japan would have to make changes so that profitability and efficient resource allocation through more competitive capital markets and more open financial institutions would make the economy more productive. I'm just saying that things might turn out "better" in the sense of accelerating the pace of liberalization and the rate of factor productivity growth so that instead of 1.5 percent or 1.6 percent growth, it's another point or point and a half higher.

Q: **So, roughly speaking, Japan's annual growth would be about that rate and China's would be on the order of 5 percent over the 15-year period.**

A: It isn't constant over the period. That's what the annualized compound rate turns out to be.

Q: **What about a country like South Korea?**

A: South Korea's growth rate is even higher—about 5.6 percent a year.

Q: **How do you see the U.S. relationship with Japan—or, for that matter, the rest of Asia—evolving over this period both economically and politically? Perhaps we can begin with China.**

A: I think there is a reasonable chance for the resumption of cross-Strait discussions on substantive matters—one of which, but not the principal one, is the one-China issue. Others include the economic issues of liberalization, reform, and market-opening as well as the rule of law. In that scenario, the outlook for the U.S.-China relationship is fairly benign, but there are other variations that would be quite dangerous.

In light of the uncertainly about those paths, the U.S.-Japan relationship is likely to be heavily influenced by the common interests of Japan and the United States in sustaining and nurturing the bilateral security treaty. The agreement to share the R&D costs of a theater missile defense system is one indicator of that.

I don't see problems with the pace of Japanese liberalization, reform, and market-opening as very likely to vitiate U.S.-Japan relations in the next 10 years as they risked doing in the 1980s and 1990s. We should encourage Japan, but I am not sure that exhorting the Japanese to do what we "know is right" for them is the best way for the United States to comport itself. At the same time, I don't see their modest, slow move in the direction that we have been talking about as a source of animosity with the United States.

Q: It may be less of a problem than it would have been 10 or 15 years ago at the time of the 1978 trade act and the smashing of Japanese radios. Have we moved beyond that?

A: I think so, but I don't think that sort of thing would have the bite that it had at the time.

Q: Of course, some people would say that it's too bad that Japan doesn't move except under some kind of threat.

A: It's up to the Japanese to find their solutions themselves. Or to make an explicit trade-off and say, well, we would rather have 1.5 percent annual growth and keep our system the way it is than to have a higher growth and change the system. They've got other problems like a declining birth rate and what to do about it with respect to female labor force participation and also in terms of relaxing immigration rules.

Q: The declining birth rate is potentially a huge budget problem?

A: A huge budget problem and perhaps a social one as well.

Q: That leaves you optimistic on some scores and less optimistic in other ways?

A: A modest pace of reform, liberalization, productivity enhancement, and growth is where I would come out.

Q: The Brookings Institution's Ed Lincoln implies in his latest book [*Troubled Times: U.S.-Japan Relations in the 1990s* (1999)] that a degree of tension in U.S.-Japan relations is healthy for inducing change in Japan.

A: I think that we are less likely to see that kind of tension because the trade gap with Japan is less important to the health of the U.S. economy than it was, assuming that the "new economy" remains strong, and because there is a greater common security interest between Japan and the United States. There may be some tension but less. But there may be more tension from the China-Japan nexus than there was, and that might provide a different kind of compulsion or responsiveness.

Postaudit

Most of what is covered in this 2000 interview remains relevant and generally accurate. This is especially true of the slow pace of deregulation, decreased factor productivity, and the growth of public investment relative to private investment.

Chapter 34

NEW THERAPIES FOR
JAPAN'S ECONOMIC SCLEROSIS
(Co-authored with Mark Buchman)

The familiar remedies for Japan's ills are not working. Last year, the inaptly-named "Big Bang" liberalization program resulted in a limited deregulation of financial services in Japan. In recent weeks, Japan's Central Bank has lowered its overnight funds rate from 1/2 to 1/4 of one percent (the comparable Federal Reserve rate is 5 1/4 percent). Still more recently, numerous *gaiatsu*-generating advisors have urged Japan to print money in abundance so as to prod Japanese consumers to divest their futons and postal savings accounts of yen in favor of a buying spree that will galvanize the depressed Japanese economy.

In fact, these therapies aggravate rather than relieve the economy's ailments.

Partial deregulation of financial services has contributed to the yen's depreciation, hardly helping Japan while harming economic recovery elsewhere in Asia. Reducing the funds rate from its already absurdly low level will have little if any positive effect in stimulating the domestic economy, because demand for both business and consumer credit is inelastic at rates as low as those prevailing before the recent further reduction. If the rate reduction has any effect at all, it is likely to be perverse by further retarding recovery prospects of the

A slightly edited version was published in **The Wall Street Journal** *on October 20, 1998 under the title "How to Save Japan From Its Own Rescue Plans."*

183

other beleaguered Asian economies. The lower Japanese rate, like the partial deregulation of financial services, increases incentives for holders of yen assets, including such giant holders as Japanese insurance companies, to flee to higher yielding foreign assets, thereby contributing to a weakened yen, hindering the competitive position of other Asian economies, and diverting Japanese capital from Asia to safer markets in the United States and Europe.

The something-for-nothing, repave-the-*ginza*-with-yen proposal is both hazardous and silly. Because the Japanese public is already disenchanted with and distrustful of politicians and bureaucrats and fearful of an uncertain future, printing money would be simplistic and ineffectual. It is as likely to make Japanese citizens "take to the streets" as they see their life-savings debased, as to make them flock to the shops in a flurry of consumer spending.

Instead of these familiar ideas, we suggest three novel ones for consideration by Mr. Obuchi and his advisors.

First, priority attention should be given to boosting the ratio of banks' capital to assets by raising the *numerator*, rather than, or in addition to, lowering the denominator. The capital-to-asset (C/A) ratio's importance arises from the minimum 8-percent standard laid down by the Bank for International Settlements as a necessary qualification for international banking activities. Some of Japan's largest city banks (for example, Sanwa and Tokyo-Mitsubishi) appear to be in reasonable compliance with this standard. It is more doubtful whether they would remain so if rigorous criteria were applied to evaluate their assets, possibly resulting in an increased requirement for loss reserves. In any event, the C/A ratios of most other Japanese banks—including, of course, the already insolvent Long Term Credit Bank—are far below the 8-percent threshold.

Most recent attention in Japan as well as that accorded by officialdom in the United States and elsewhere has focused entirely on the denominator of this C/A ratio. So, using "public" money (i.e., ultimately provided by Japanese taxpayers) has been repeatedly urged to reduce the banks' holdings of weak assets by subrogating them to the government (along the lines of the Resolution Trust Corporation in the U.S. savings and loan debacle of the late 1980s).

Instead, the capital of Japanese banks should be enlarged by floating substantial additional equities for purchase by the Japanese public, as well as by foreign investors. To be sure, this would dilute existing equity holdings. But, by widening the relatively thin market for bank equities, which largely represent cross-holdings among other banks and large companies, this measure would inject new capital into bank balance sheets by attracting private capital from both domestic and foreign sources.

Second, the Bank of Japan should *raise* its short-term rate (reversing the 25-basis point reduction referred to earlier) by a few percentage points. One reason for this unconventional proposal is to attract private savings into banks by raising the deposit rates received by depositors. A second reason is to reduce incentives for yen flight created by the gap between low interest rates in Japan, and higher ones in the United States and Europe. Yen flight is the underlying explanation for the persistent anomaly of a weak Japanese yen co-existing with a surging Japanese current account surplus—two phenomena that do not normally co-habit. The large rate differential drives capital outflows from Japan to foreign equity and bond markets, results in a weakened yen which, while strengthening Japanese exports, aggravates protectionism in the U.S. and elsewhere, makes life more difficult for other Asian economies (especially Korea and Southeast Asia), and might move China closer toward devaluation while blaming Japan if it does so. Removing, or at least reducing, this interest rate differential can help reverse this perverse cycle.

Our proposed interest rate boost can be accomplished by sales of some of the government's 300 trillion yen (about $2.2 trillion) of government debt to domestic and foreign buyers, thus depressing bond values and increasing interest rates.

Paradoxically, this measure will not have deflationary consequences in Japan. Credit in Japan is, for the most part, extended on a relationship-driven basis, in which interest rates don't play a significant role, except to the extent that they favor export industries, thereby further aggravating the cycle referred to above. If and as the yen strengthens, import prices in Japan should decline somewhat and consumer demand will respond accordingly.

These measures should be part of a serious effort to replace Japan's perennial export-led growth strategy with what one of the authors has termed an "import-accommodating" strategy through market-opening policies that are neutral with respect to exports and imports.

This "import accommodating" strategy (see *Wall Street Journal,* May 20, 1998) is the third of our suggested therapies. Intended to make Japan's markets more open, accessible, and competitive, it would include several elements:

• rapid reduction and eventual removal of preferential policies for export firms and industries, and of non-tariff barriers that impede import competition;

• permanent reduction of individual and corporate income taxes to levels at or below those in the United States and other healthy economies, as well as elimination of the domestic consumption tax that was introduced several years ago.

Such measures can help revive a Japanese economy whose predicament is the result of four decades of unremitting mercantilism designed and coordinated by its elite Finance and International Trade bureaucracy, implemented by its favored export industries, endorsed by its political class, and accepted by a passive Japanese public. Ultimately, rejuvenating the sclerotic economy depends on raising the productivity and profitability of capital in Japan by opening and expanding its domestic market. In turn, this depends on removing the pervasive barriers inhibiting market access by new firms and producers, whether Japanese or foreign.

Lately, and in part as a result of a profusion of rhetoric from an odd assortment of pundits, including Mohamad Mahathir, George Soros, Yevgeny Primakov, and Paul Krugman, it has become fashionable to harangue against the miscarriages of free markets. Japan is a compelling counter example: revival of Japan's economy depends on sustained efforts to move its economy away from restricted markets and toward a freer, more open, and competitive market-governed system.

Postaudit

Sometimes advice that seems even more sensible ex post *than it did* ex ante *seems* ex post *to have been heeded even less than might have been expected* ex ante! *What is suggested in this article illustrates this point. The following chapter perhaps explains why this has occurred.*

Chapter 35

JAPAN'S COMFORTABLE STAGNATION

Economic stagnation in Japan is uniquely compatible with generally prevalent comfort, which is a major reason why stagnation is likely to endure. Underlying this endurance is the fact that zero economic growth or very slow growth in Japan still implies rising per capita income because Japan's population will soon begin to decline.

In the 1970s and 1980s, Japan was the economic wonder of the industrial world, recording the highest annual growth rate among all developed economies throughout this period. Its annual growth averaged above 4 percent, transforming Japan into the world's second largest economy. This remarkable record provoked a heated debate in policy and academic circles about explanations for the economic "miracle," as well as prognoses that Japan would either surpass the U.S. economy, or at least buy substantial parts of it!

During the 1990s and the first years of the 21st century, Japan's rapid growth was replaced by protracted economic stagnation, evoking hardly less wonder, and a corresponding debate about explanations for this economic deterioration, and its implications for Japan's future performance. This debate is tinged with irony because many commentators—in both policy and academic circles—who had previously offered convincing explanations for Japan's success, subsequently offered equally firm pronouncements about its more recent economic failures, having forgotten their categorical assertions about Japan's enduring success in the prior decades.

---

*A slightly edited version was published in **The Los Angeles Times** on February 24, 2002 under the title "The Wages of Comfort."*

The Japanese "miracle" of the 1970s and 1980s was the result of several mutually reinforcing factors: high rates of savings and of private (if "guided") capital formation; a skilled, vigorous, and growing labor force; a positive rate of productivity growth for both capital and labor; and accommodating monetary policy which provided credit on favorable terms to aggressive, export-oriented industries and firms, especially in the automotive and electronic fields.

In combination, these factors overshadowed the accumulating inefficiencies resulting from a protected domestic market and an industrial policy in which government and the bureaucracy (notably, the Ministry of Finance and the Ministry of International Trade and Industry), rather than competitive markets, determined how and to what purposes resources were allocated.

Japan's stagnation in the 1990s and the first years of the 21st century has been driven by an equally potent set of forces, in large measure derived from the same factors contributing to the economic miracle of the 1970s and 1980s. These factors include:

- An industrial system principally driven by considerations of economies of scale, increasing market share, and export growth, with profitability viewed as less important in determining resource allocations and the development of particular industries and firms.

- A banking system pervaded by huge non-performing loans and weak balance sheets resulting from Japan's distorted industrial base and the credit misallocations associated with it.

- A regulatory system marked by the heavy hand of government and protectionism, limiting free entry and market access both within Japan and from potentially competitive firms outside, in the process stifling entrepreneurship and innovation. (Recent RAND work on economic "openness" found that Japan ranked far below the economies of both the U.S. and Germany, and about on a par with China and Korea, in its profusion of non-tariff restrictions permeating the economy and impeding market access by foreign businesses.)

Reflecting as well as contributing to these negative drivers, the ratio of Japanese government investment to private investment nearly doubled between the 1980s and 1990s, and the absolute level of private investment declined by more than 12 percent in the same period. Correspondingly, the amount of new capital formation required per unit of added output more than doubled, while the annual rise in productivity of both capital and labor plummeted from just over 0.5 percent in the 1980s, to a *negative* figure of 2.1 percent in the 1990s.

To mitigate these circumstances, Japan's reforms have been somewhere between bland and modest. These efforts have included loosened monetary policies with near zero interest rates and government bailout funding for the major banks to strengthen their fragile balance sheets and encourage new lending; increased levels of public spending, thereby expanding Japan's already large public debt, currently estimated between two and four times its GDP (the corresponding U.S. debt figure is less than half of GDP); and a modest degree of deregulation allowing foreign investors to acquire Japanese assets in some fields.

Most observers, myself included, think these efforts are inadequate. Without more drastic deregulation, Japan's near stagnation is likely to continue. RAND forecasts envisage Japan's annual growth in the first decade of the 21st century as likely to hover between zero and slightly above one percent annually.

Despite these trends, Japan is hardly in a "crisis" condition. It remains wealthy, with per capita GDP among the highest in the world. Sales in Japan of luxury consumer goods carrying the prestige labels of Vuiton, Gucci, Hermes, and Courvoisier continue to be strong, the standard of living of Japan's 127 million people is among the highest in the industrial world, its current account surplus ($117 billion in 2000), is the world's largest, as is its nearly $400 billion in foreign exchange reserves, almost twice those of second-place China. Its pledge of assistance for rebuilding Afghanistan ($500 million) is larger than that of the United States or the European Union.

Moreover, Japan's cities are generally among the world's cleanest and safest. Public services are reliable and efficient by comparison with those elsewhere in the developed world. (When one steps beyond the gate of an arriving flight in the Tokyo or Osaka airports, within five seconds a noiseless and speedy shuttle arrives to move one to another terminal for a connecting flight, a sharp contrast to

what one found in U.S. airports before September 11 and, more un-
derstandably, since then). And, even with low growth or zero growth
in GDP, Japan's per capita income will continue to rise because
Japan's population will begin to decline in the first decade of the 21st
century; declining population will, by 2010, *raise* per capita income
by nearly 1 percent in each subsequent five-year period, even assuming that Japan's GDP remains unchanged!

Thus, stagnation in Japan is compatible with a high level of consumer
well-being and comfort, as it would not be in, say, the United States
or the European Union. This comfort level reduces pressures for real
structural reform to reinvigorate the Japanese economy by pervasive
deregulation, weeding out or consolidation of unprofitable firms and
precarious banks through bankruptcies and acquisitions, and creating a new business environment to encourage rather than discourage
Japanese entrepreneurs, as well as foreign investors. Whether internal political pressure will be able to alter this "stagnation with
comfort" scenario is doubtful. A more likely stimulus, if indeed any
ensues, may be provided by China. If China's economic and/or
military power provide strong evidence that China will eclipse Japan
in the Asian regional context, the resulting shock in Japan may have
consequences equivalent to those which occurred following the Meiji
restoration in the late 19th century.

Postaudit

*Whether Japan is more likely to respond to internal pressures (as
many putative experts believe), or to an external shock (as I suggest),
or to continue its comfortable stagnation more or less indefinitely,
remains in contention.*

Chapter 36

HOW TO DEFEND JAPAN WHILE "ENGAGING" CHINA

In the next few weeks, the crucial dilemma facing U.S. security policy in the Asia-Pacific region will be highlighted when the new guidelines for the Japan American Security Alliance (JASA) are finalized on September 24th, and one month later China's president Jiang Zemin arrives in Washington for his first state visit with President Clinton.

The dilemma arises because the two principal elements of U.S. security policy in the region—"revitalizing" JASA, and "engagement" of China—are in conflict with one another. Advancing the first retards the second. The two impending events are reflective of this conflict.

The conflict springs from several sources: inherent ambiguity of the term "engagement," and Chinese suspicions that it is really a euphemism for a U.S. strategy of "containment" designed to keep China's ascending power in check; Chinese concerns that a revitalized JASA is a part of this strategy, and may weigh (adversely, from China's standpoint) in the balance of forces affecting Taiwan's future; China's fears that—intentionally or inadvertently—revitalizing JASA runs the risk of re-igniting Japanese militarism; and residual Chinese resentment of Japan's depredations in Manchuria in the 1930s, its atrocities in World War II, and its continued unwillingness to formally acknowledge its guilt for this history (as Germany has long since done).

---

*A slightly edited version was published in **The Wall Street Journal** on September 24, 1997 under the same title.*

While the precise import of renewing and revitalizing JASA is still to be worked out, its various facets are likely to include an expanded role for Japan's naval forces in protecting sea lines of communication (SLOCs) extending from Japan, closer linkages between American and Japanese command, control, and communication (C3) systems, closer coupling of logistic support and maintenance, and collaborative R&D activities perhaps encompassing theater missile defense technologies. (JASA's role, if any, in the event of a possible Taiwan contingency is likely to be deliberately omitted from the new guidelines.)

Any of these measures, let alone all of them, will heighten previously existing Chinese suspicions that U.S. pronouncements about "engagement" are just empty rhetoric. The term's inherent ambiguity doesn't help matters—for example, in one context it implies an abiding commitment of unity, while in another a commitment to combat (recall Napoleon's dictum about military strategy: "*on s'engage, et puis on voit*"). Chinese suspicions are not allayed by the fact that the Chinese ideograph most closely approximating the term "engagement" is the same as that which connotes "containment."

So, from China's standpoint, the reality of actions provided for or planned in revitalizing JASA contrast unfavorably with the vagueness and elusiveness of the "engagement" rhetoric espoused by the United States.

From the contrasting U.S. standpoint, Japan's Self-Defense Forces are small in size and limited in capabilities, so upgrading them and linking them more closely to U.S. forward-based forces is amply warranted if Japan is to assume a fairer share of the joint alliance burden. Indeed, Japan's military spending, at just under 1 percent of GDP compared with over 3 percent in the United States, is the lowest military spending share of any of America's allies in Asia or Europe. From this standpoint, revitalizing JASA is both legitimate and indeed overdue.

Clearly, these sharply contrasting views are a reflection of the familiar axiom: "Where you stand depends on where you sit." But the resultant of the different views is that revitalizing JASA collides with "engagement" of China.

This brings to mind a somewhat similar collision between two precepts of U.S. security policy in Europe. There, revitalizing NATO through its eastward "enlargement" to embrace Poland, Hungary, and the Czech Republic has collided with efforts to improve relations with Russia and to encourage its continued reform and progress. In Europe, the means by which this collision is being cushioned, and perhaps averted, may also have applicability in Asia, notwithstanding major differences between the two regions.

On May 27, 1997, the Secretary General of NATO and Russia's president signed the "Founding Act on Mutual Relations, Cooperation, and Security between Russia and NATO." The Act's principal aims and commitments include: "Development on the basis of transparency . . . of a strong . . . and equal partnership . . . and cooperation to strengthen security and stability in the Euro-Atlantic area, refraining from the use of force . . . , mutual transparency in creating and implementing defense policy and military doctrines."

To pursue these aims, the Founding Act has established a "Permanent Joint Council" (PJC) to meet regularly and to consult on "issues of common interest related to security and stability . . . , arms control, . . . expanded cooperation between the respective military establishments, . . . and developing mutually agreed cooperative projects in defense-related economic, environmental, and scientific fields."

To be sure, some of this represents rhetoric and symbolism whose implementation lies in the future. However, the precedent can be adapted in Asia to mitigate the conflict between revitalizing JASA on the one hand, and engagement of China on the other.

Toward this end, it would be timely for the United States and China to enter into a compact that might be called "The Enabling Act on Mutual Relations, Cooperation, and Security between China and the United States" that would envisage establishment of a Permanent Joint Council between China and the United States. The Council's purposes would include regular consultations on issues of common interest related to security and stability in the Asia-Pacific region, exchange of information on planned military exercises, provision of military-to-military exchanges for training and informational activities, transparency in defense policy and defense budgeting, and consideration of other activities that may be jointly agreed upon by China and the United States.

The forthcoming meeting between Presidents Clinton and Jiang in Washington at the end of October provides an historic opportunity to begin discussions of such an "Enabling Act" and a Permanent Joint Council between China and the United States. As an expression of purpose and intent, inclusion of this subject in the meeting's agenda and communiqué would represent a major accomplishment even if, as in Europe, translating it into something concrete and effective remains for the future.

It is likely that, in the years ahead, the United States and China will experience frictions and strife between them. Creating such an Enabling Act and establishing a Permanent Joint Council involving the leadership of the PLA and the U.S. military establishment would be valuable contributions toward easing such friction and avoiding misunderstandings in advance of or during possible crisis situations.

Postaudit

The context of this chapter is somewhat time-bound. However, the general issue of how the United States can and should maintain a (perhaps moving) balance in its relations with a Japanese ally and a sometimes friendly and sometimes less friendly China remains relevant and unresolved.

Chapter 37

WHEN A BALANCE OF POWER CAN BE DESTABILIZING

What will determine whether the Asia-Pacific region will experience peace and stability, or conflict and disorder, in the next decade? Most responses to the question take either of two forms: broad and general answers (for example, the outcome will depend on continuation or interruption of the region's dynamic economic growth, on whether or not the Asia-Pacific region proceeds toward integration into the world economy, and on the character of China's post-Deng leadership); or specific answers that focus on particular issues or disputes in the region (for example, the status of Taiwan, how the "one-China-two systems" formula plays out, whether the disputes over the Spratly and Senkaku-Diaoyu Islands flare up, and the perennial threat on the Korean peninsula).

All of these considerations are relevant. However, none is likely to have as much effect on the region's outlook for stability or conflict as another consideration that overarches all of the others: namely, a particular geo-political and geo-strategic perspective that China's leaders and many of its intellectuals (including many "liberal" ones) share, and at times vigorously espouse. This perspective can be summarized in the following syllogism:

*A slightly edited version was published in **The Asian Wall Street Journal** on December 3, 1996 under the title "Don't Give In to China's Tantrums."*

1.   Peace and stability in the Asia-Pacific region depend on a balance of power among the three major powers in the region: the United States, China and Japan.

2.   At the present time, and in the immediate future, this "balance" is profoundly *unbalanced* because China is so much weaker than the United States and Japan—economically, militarily, and in terms of international diplomatic and political "clout."

3.   Therefore, peace and stability in the region depend on a substantial increase in China's relative power (in all the dimensions referred to above), relative to the United States and Japan, so that the triangular relationship among them will be more balanced.

This strategic vision is shared not only among China's top leaders, but among intellectuals and academics many of whom are considered, and consider themselves, to be both "liberal" and favorably disposed to the United States. According to this view, developments that contribute to the increased strength of China—relative to other members of this strategic regional triangle—should be welcomed and even encouraged. Conversely, whatever might delay or obstruct this adjustment should be opposed or eschewed.

China's balance-of-power perspective has direct operational consequences. For example, in China's eyes, this view justifies enhancement of China's military capabilities to protect its 10,000 miles of land border and 3,000 miles of coastline facing neighbors who have not always been seen as friendly to China. Moreover, China's attitude toward the forward military presence of the United States in the Asia-Pacific region, and in particular its attitude toward the U.S. security alliance with Japan, depend significantly on the balance-of-power idea. To the extent that the U.S. alliance with Japan has a braking effect on expansion of Japan's military capabilities—including both conventional force modernization and theater missile defense—China not only accepts, but endorses, the U.S.-Japan alliance. But, if and when the alliance seems to encourage Japan to acquire greater military capabilities and to assume greater alliance responsibilities, as the Chinese plausibly inferred from the April 1996 joint communiqué of President Clinton and Prime Minister Hashimoto, then China's attitude toward the alliance becomes querulous and antagonistic.

The reason China's balance-of-power perspective is so crucial in its effect on the outlook for peace or conflict, stability or disorder, in the Asia-Pacific region, lies in the familiar aphorism that "where you stand depends on where you sit," and its less-familiar corollary that "what you see depends on where you stand." From Beijing's standpoint, the balance-of-power perspective is entirely realistic: what it sees is the decidedly unbalanced relationship among the three apexes of the triangle. From the standpoints of others in the region— from Tokyo to Seoul, to Washington, to Hanoi, to Singapore, to Kuala Lumpur, to Jakarta, and even to New Delhi—the existing imbalance, and especially the forward presence and military predominance of the United States, is a reassuring harbinger of predictability, peace, and stability in the region. Conversely, a substantial accretion in China's relative power, especially military power, is seen as potentially threatening. Among the other countries of the region, China's balance-of-power view of the world provides a strong reason for upgrading their own military capabilities, and developing a security structure in the region that will either counter or co-opt China's weight. One result is that the Asia-Pacific region has become the largest regional buyer in the current $25 billion a year international weapons market.

In this dynamic relationship, China has major advantages. Its GDP growth rate, though likely to slow somewhat from the double-digit pace of the past decade, will probably be two or three times that of the United States and Japan. Its willingness to allocate resources for military spending will be greater than that of the United States or Japan and, according to recent RAND calculations, its acquisition of new military systems will probably increase relative to that of the United States and Japan over the next decade. The paradox is that the more China moves to create what it regards as a "balance" of power, the less favorable will be the outlook for stability in the region, as well as for China's own progress, prosperity, and place in the world.

What the United States should do in these circumstances is limited, but certainly not negligible. Perhaps the best course for the United States to follow is to prevent China from gaining concessions through the use of force (as was demonstrated by the U.S. response to China's missile launchings in the Taiwan Strait in March of 1996), while acknowledging and even adjusting to China's interests when force is eschewed (appropriately conditioned membership in WTO, may be an example). The United States should be prepared to check the misuse of power by China, while avoiding any temptation to misuse or overuse power itself. The less China gains through the threat or use of force, while managing to gain some without it, perhaps the more will China be motivated to pursue the non-military dimensions of its enhanced status, and the less motivated to pursue the military dimensions.

Postaudit

As a member of the U.S.-led post–9/11 coalition, China's relationship to the United States has changed since this essay was written in 1996. However, the thrust of the piece—that is, balancing China's evolving views of its own balance of power—remains relevant.

Chapter 38

MANAGING THE COSTS OF KOREAN REUNIFICATION—*IF* IT OCCURS

Prospects for eventual reunification of North and South Korea appear brighter than at any time in the past several decades. Yet it is premature, if not naïve, to assume that reunification will occur smoothly, let alone peacefully.

To be sure, the recent signs are encouraging, as well as unusual: the much publicized embrace by the two Presidents Kim and their amicable discussions in June, followed by exchanges of visits between 100 selected North and South Korean families, by the release by South Korea of several dozen convicted North Korean spies, and by the joint appearance of the South and North Korean Olympic teams in Sydney on September 21.

Nevertheless, in the past there have been numerous occasions where indications of an impending relaxation of tensions were followed by blatant North Korean acts of hostility and violence, including sabotage in the South, attempted assassinations, and infiltration of guerrilla units into the South.

If this explosive pattern from the past is not repeated this time around, one issue that still might—but should not—be allowed to impede progress toward reunification is fear by South Korea (and its ally, the United States), as well as exaggerated expectations by the North, of the enormous costs to South Korea (benefactions, from the

---

A slightly edited version was published in **The Asian Wall Street Journal** *on October 3, 2000 under the title "How Much for One Korea?"*

standpoint of North Korea) that reunification would entail. In fact, contrary to much conventional lore and questionable calculations on the subject, the costs of reunification can be held within moderate bounds by a combination of sensible negotiations and effective management of the reunification process.

In the recent past, the costs of Korean reunification have been plausibly, but misleadingly, estimated by several sources including the World Bank to be as high as $2–3 trillion, about five or six times South Korea's gross domestic product! Such exorbitant economic costs, quite apart from the enormous political and social problems that reunification would present, have made reunification at any time in the next few decades seem chimerical.

The seeming plausibility of these estimates has been driven by the experience of German reunification in the past decade, and its huge (still continuing, and originally underestimated) costs. At first glance it might appear that the costs of Korean reunification would impose even larger relative burdens than those that materialized in the German case. For example, the population of North Korea is about half that of the South, while that of East Germany was only one-quarter that of West Germany. Moreover, per capita GDP in North Korea is perhaps only one-fifth to one-tenth that of South Korea, while per capita GDP in East Germany was believed in 1991 to be about two-thirds to three-quarters that of West Germany. (In the event, the East German per capita GDP actually turned out to be more like one-quarter that in West Germany, hence not that different from the comparison between North and South Korea.)

So, if the relative income disparity and the relative population magnitudes between North and South Korea are assumed to be much larger that the corresponding comparisons in East and West Germany, the plausible inference has been drawn that the costs of Korean reunification would be relatively even greater than the costs actually experienced in the German case—"plausible," but un-warranted.

Several offsetting considerations lead to quite a different conclusion.

If the process of reunification in Korea is negotiated sensibly and managed carefully, the ensuing cost burden imposed on the South and its allies can be limited to a sum that is less than one-tenth of the conventional estimates!

The principal offsets include the resource savings and reallocations to be gleaned by substantial military downsizing, as well as by prudently limiting the economic goals that reunification should seek:

- North Korea continues to support a huge military establishment: 1.1 million men in its regular armed forces plus about four times that number in its reserves, as well as a large defense industry which undergirds these forces and generates North Korea's principal exports. The economic burden this imposes amounts to between 30 and 40 percent of the country's GDP. (In East Germany, the military consisted mainly of Soviet forces, largely representing a cost burden on the Soviet Union not on East Germany itself.) If and as progress toward reunification in Korea occurs, substantial savings and reallocations of resources can be realized by a commensurate downsizing of the North Korean military establishment. My initial calculations suggest that savings from this source should be between 13 and 15 billion U.S. dollars annually, provided downsizing of North Korean military forces is negotiated as an integral part of the reunification process.

- Additional, but smaller, savings can also be realized by a reduction of South Korea's own military forces of 600,000 men. These savings could be between 2 and 3 billion dollars annually, envisaging a total military force on the peninsula of perhaps 400,000, instead of the 1.7 million armed forces that currently face one another across the 54th parallel.

- While resources can be saved by a significant military build-*down*, the quantity of resources needed for North Korea's economic build-*up* can be bounded by establishing reasonable, limited, and realistic targets for reunification. For example, economic targets should be considered that are sufficient, but not excessive, for preventing a large population flow from North to South Korea. (Incidentally, Korea's location and topography make the goal of controlling excessive population flows much more practicable than in the German case.) With this goal in mind, it would be reasonable, for example, to aim at a doubling of per capita income in the North over a five- to seven-year period. It would be quite unnecessary as well as unreasonable to seek to equalize per capita income levels between North and South in any short period of time. (It is worth recalling that, for political reasons, German reunification was launched with overambitious economic and financial targets: for example, equalizing the par values of the ostmark and the deutschmark, standardizing the package of social entitlements between the East and the West, etc.) If the reasonable goals mentioned above are established for Korean reunification at the outset of the process, the total capital costs of achieving them should not exceed four or five times North Korea's estimated GDP.

So, setting the resource reallocations from the military build-down in both North and South Korea—about $75 billion over a five-year period—against a rough estimate of the costs of reconstruction in the North of $200 billion (assuming a capital-to-output ratio of four; hence, four times North Korea's GDP), would still leave a large but much more manageable cost of $125 billion. It is not unreasonable to assume that, say, half this sum could come from private foreign capital motivated by profit considerations. The residual would require public capital transfers—bilaterally from South Korea, Japan, and the United States, and multilaterally from the World Bank Group and the Asian Development Bank—of between $60 and $65 billion over a five-year period.

Although these numbers are substantial, they are about the same as the bailout funds provided to South Korea to relieve its short-term financial crisis in 1997 and 1998.

The costs of Korean reunification are much more manageable than has usually been assumed. Exaggerated estimates of these costs should not be allowed to hinder or delay reunification.

Postaudit

While some of the parameters have changed, the essential points about how the costs of Korean reunification can be held to manageable amounts remain valid.

ABOUT THE AUTHOR

Charles Wolf, Jr., formerly Dean of the RAND Graduate School, is a senior economic adviser and corporate fellow in international economics at RAND and professor in the RAND Graduate School. He received his BS and PhD degrees in economics from Harvard. From 1967 until June 1981, he was head of RAND's Economics Department, and thereafter was director of RAND research in international economics.

Dr. Wolf is a Senior Research Fellow at the Hoover Institution, and a director of Capital Income Builder Fund, Inc. and Capital World Growth and Income Fund, Inc. He is a member of the advisory boards of the UCLA Management School's Center for International Business Education and Research, the *Independent Institute*, the journal *Society*, and the editorial board of the *Korean Journal of Defense Analysis*. He is a member of the American Economic Association, the Econometric Society, the Council on Foreign Relations, and the International Institute for Strategic Studies. Dr. Wolf has served with the Department of State, and has taught at Cornell, the University of California at Berkeley, UCLA, and Nuffield College, Oxford. He is the author or co-author of numerous journal articles and two dozen books including *Markets or Governments: Choosing Between Imperfect Alternatives* (MIT Press, 1993*), Promoting Democracy and Free Markets in Eastern Europe* (1992), *The Economic Pivot in a Political Context* (1997), *Asian Economic Trends and Their Security Implications* (2000), and *China, the United States and the Global Economy,* (2001).